"One of David Hawkins's clients said sh[e]
have an average marriage. She wanted m[ore]
book worth reading. *90 Days to a Fanta[stic]*
on or try to solve the problems of troubl[ed]
Dr. Hawkins offers a twelve-week progr[am]
improve marriage—any marriage."

CECIL MURPHEY
Author/coauthor of over 100 books, including *Gifted Hands:
The Ben Carson Story* and *90 Minutes in Heaven*

"Falling in love is easy. Maintaining the passion after you've taken
your marriage vows is harder. But you can do it! In this hope-filled
book, Dr. David Hawkins provides a twelve-week plan that will
help reignite the spark in your relationship. A valuable resource
for any couple wanting more from their marriage."

DR. GREG AND ERIN SMALLEY
www.smalleymarriage.com

"Dr. David Hawkins is warm, articulate, knowledgeable, and
passionate about helping people. His latest book, *90 Days to
a Fantastic Marriage*, is practical, well-written, and overflowing
with the knowledge and insight we desperately need to rekindle
the embers of today's broken and mundane marriages."

DEBRA MAFFETT
Host, *The Harvest Show*

"Dr. David Hawkins writes with penetrating insight and
practicality. His entertaining and engaging style will make you
smile, laugh, and reflect . . . and, most important, give you the
tools you need to build a stronger marriage."

BILL PERKINS
Founder and CEO, Million Mighty Men
Author, *When Good Men Are Tempted* and *6 Rules Every Man
Must Break*

"*90 Days to a Fantastic Marriage* delivers exactly that! Evidence of Dr. Hawkins's deepest desire to empower couples, inspire individuals, and restore marriages is on every page along with practical and passionate steps to accomplish it. The way Dr. Hawkins challenges us to embrace our spouses as soul mates will definitely lead to a checkmate on the chessboard of marriage. I particularly found that his weekly encouragement to strike out on new adventures in my marriage is bringing me to a place of renewed friendship and intimate satisfaction with my husband. This is a must-read for all couples, not just those in trouble."

LINDA GOLDFARB
Radio and Web TV personality
Founder/CEO of Live Powerfully Now Ministries

*90 Days to a Fantastic Marriage*

# 90 DAYS TO A FANTASTIC Marriage

*How to Bring Out the*
*Soul Mate in Your Mate*

## DR. DAVID HAWKINS

Tyndale House Publishers, Inc.
Carol Stream, Illinois

Visit Tyndale's exciting Web site at www.tyndale.com

www.yourrelationshipdoctor.com

*TYNDALE* and Tyndale's quill logo are registered trademarks of Tyndale House Publishers, Inc.

*90 Days to a Fantastic Marriage: How to Bring Out the Soul Mate in Your Mate*

Copyright © 2009 by David Hawkins. All rights reserved.

Cover photo copyright © Polka Dot Images/jupiterimages. All rights reserved.

Designed by Erik M. Peterson

The names and identifying details of the couples whose stories appear in this book have been changed to protect their privacy.

**Library of Congress Cataloging-in-Publication Data**

Hawkins, David, date.
   90 days to a fantastic marriage : how to bring out the soul mate in your mate /
David Hawkins.
      p. cm.
   Includes bibliographical references.
   ISBN 978-1-4143-2324-4 (sc)
   1. Marriage—Religious aspects—Christianity.   2. Man-woman relationships—Religious
aspects—Christianity.   I. Title.   II. Title: Ninety days to a fantastic marriage.
   BV835.H3775 2009
   248.8'44—dc22                                                                    2009005466

Printed in the United States of America

15  14  13  12  11  10  09

7   6   5   4   3   2   1

This book is dedicated to every couple ready
to transform their attitudes in an effort to
rekindle the romance in their relationship.

# CONTENTS

# ACKNOWLEDGMENTS

I want to first thank Tyndale House Publishers for inviting me and my wife, Christie, to be part of the family. Our time together in Orlando was wonderful, as your hospitality made us feel very privileged.

I want to specifically thank Jan Long Harris for meeting with my wife and me on numerous occasions and helping me articulate the message of this book. Thank you, Jan, for your creative energy, for your brainstorming ability, and for taking a chance on me and this book.

Thanks also go to Kim Miller for reading the book with care, tightening my writing, and walking me through suggestions to make it a stronger book. Thank you, Kim, for your work on this book.

This book, finally, is lovingly dedicated to my wife, Christie. While many other editorial touches to the manuscript have made it a better book, it is Christie's enthusiasm and unfaltering positive approach to life that makes this book what it is. Christie believes in everyone, it seems, but moreover believes in me. She also believes in each one of you! Thank you, sweetie, for loving me and for being an integral voice in this book.

# PROLOGUE:
# MAKING NEW CHOICES

*And now these three remain: faith, hope and love.*
*But the greatest of these is love.*
—1 Corinthians 13:13

"I can't believe it, Dr. Hawkins. I just had to call and tell you what's happened."

No sooner had I picked up my ringing office phone than a woman began speaking excitedly. She hadn't even greeted me or given her name. I scrambled to place her voice and figure out why she was calling.

"Who is this?" I asked.

"Oh, I'm sorry. This is Susie Johnson. You saw me and my husband, Dillon, last year. We were caught in a vicious cycle of fighting, and you helped us learn to communicate. At the end of our final session, you invited us to contact you again to let you know how we're doing."

"Go ahead," I said, still trying to place the name. "What's happened?"

"When we came to see you, I just wanted my husband back. I wanted the relationship we had back when we were first married. But I got far more than I bargained for!"

"Really?" I said. "Tell me what you mean."

"So you do remember us?" she asked.

"Of course, I remember you," I said, piecing together my work with them.

When they had arrived for their first appointment, Susie struck me as reserved. Dillon, her husband, had been more animated, greeting me warmly with a smile and firm handshake. After we were all seated, I asked why they had come.

"There's nothing really wrong with our marriage," Susie said. "But there has got to be more. We don't fight, but we don't seem to have much passion either."

Here was a woman going for the gusto. Unwilling to settle for a mundane, stable but boring marriage, she wanted more and she was willing to rock the boat a bit to get it.

"What do you think, Dillon?" I had asked.

"I agree with Susie. We've gotten too busy with our work and raising a family, and we have kind of lost each other. I want the spark back too."

My memory of that first meeting was interrupted by Susie's voice over the phone. "I remember thinking, just before we came for our first appointment, that maybe all couples reach a point when they just have to slog through their marriages."

"And I remember telling you," I said, "how glad I was that you'd come in when you did. Too many couples wait far too long, letting their love slip away and resentments grow. That clearly wasn't a problem with you two yet. You had a lot to build on."

"When you and Dillon came to see me a year or so ago, you guys said you wanted to strengthen your marriage. Things are better, I take it?"

"They're not just better, Dr. David. This is going to sound like an infomercial, but it's true. We came to you as mates and left as soul mates. It's incredible."

"I'm curious," I said. "What do you mean when you say 'soul mate'?"

"Hmm. I'll have to think about that," Susie said, pausing for a moment. "It's not any one thing. It's a lot of little things."

I smiled. When we'd started meeting, I'd stressed the need to examine the unhealthy ways Susie and Dillon had been relating to one another so we could understand why their marriage felt stale. I had to zero in on those patterns—like criticizing, interrupting, and tuning one another out—that were pulling them apart.

"So what little things are different?" I said, taking a few notes as she began talking.

"Let me mention a couple of things that come to mind," she said, sounding pleased that I had asked her to elaborate on their current relationship.

"Just last week, my parents were visiting. When my mom told me—as she has on her last ten visits—that I really should rearrange my cupboards so my dishes would be closer to the table, Dillon just smiled at me. I knew he was saying, 'It's okay. I love you.' Then later, when the four of us took a walk around the block, he just grabbed my hand spontaneously. He never would have done that a year ago. We even catch ourselves saying the same things at the same time, and then we smile and say, 'We're soul mates.'"

Susie paused for another moment and then continued. "You know, I haven't really sat back and thought about all the little things that make us soul mates. But when I think about it, there are many things we do now that we never used to do."

"Susie, what you're telling me is what I tell every couple that comes to see me. Any couple willing to exchange destructive ways of relating for positive ways can bring the excitement back into a relationship. It's great to hear you sounding so content. I presume Dillon is happy as well."

"Oh," she said, laughing. "I think he'd tell you he's very happy. What man doesn't want a woman who thinks she's married to a prince?"

Does Susie's story sound like a fairy tale? Maybe a Hollywood love story? When you hear the word *soul mates*, are you more likely to think of Tom Hanks and Meg Ryan in *Sleepless in Seattle* than a couple like Susie and Dillon, a husband and wife with ordinary jobs living in an ordinary town who had come to me because their marriage had become, well, too ordinary?

The good news is that most of us are far more like Susie and Dillon than Meg and Tom. Our lives may seem pretty average to us, but our marriages don't have to be. Susie and Dillon's marriage improved once they discovered that finding their soul mate was a matter of uncovering, recovering, and discovering what had drawn them together in the first place. It required work and intention. It was more of a journey than a destination.

You may be wondering if you have the time and energy to invest in your relationship. You may be thinking, *With everything else my spouse and I are dealing with—pressures on the job, issues with our kids, struggles with finances—why is it worth investing time in trying to become soul mates? And what does it mean to be a soul mate, anyway?*

These are good questions, and there are solid answers. In fact, I discovered the hard way the extraordinary cost of drifting along after my first marriage ended in divorce. Both my ex-wife and I had gotten caught up in our careers and family and forgot the importance of keeping the relationship between the two of us strong.

As a result of that heartache, I resolved that if I married again I would make that relationship a priority. I'm so grateful for my wife, Christie, who desires a soul mate marriage just as much as I do. I know from my experience that there is nothing more satisfying than enjoying a rich relationship. Nothing will make you feel quite as complete as being completely loved by your mate. To be treasured, prized, and appreciated is part of being a soul mate—and you'd probably be willing to give nearly anything to have those qualities in your marital relationship.

## The Best Intentions

Finding your soul mate is not a matter of chance, serendipity, or luck. It isn't about making sure you're in the right place at the right time. You don't drop the one you're with to go looking for that perfect match—he or she is sitting across the dining room table from you, waiting to be discovered. The primary ingredient required to bring out the best in your mate—which is the basis of becoming a soul mate—is intentionality.

Finding your soul mate is as simple as deciding to alter your behavior in ways that will enable your mate to become your soul mate. Starting with one step, one intentional action, you can encourage your mate to be your soul mate. Choosing to bring out the best in each other, day after day, week after week, revolutionizes a relationship.

In *90 Days to a Fantastic Marriage: How to Bring Out the Soul Mate in Your Mate*, I'm asking you to commit for twelve weeks to a process designed to help you discover and nurture the soul of your mate—and enable your mate to do the same. This book is packed with ideas to transform your marriage by bringing out the best in your spouse—and in you. Each week, you'll learn a new skill to help you draw closer to your spouse, using the tools that have helped thousands of couples transform their relationships, just as Susie and Dillon did.

Now I realize your marriage may be broken. Perhaps your spouse has expressed no interest in drawing closer to you. If so, you may have resigned yourself to a lifeless marriage, expecting nothing to change. Maybe you've even thought of leaving your mate.

I'm going to offer you a third option based on this simple truth: If just one spouse wants to change a stale or mundane marriage, he or she has the power to start the transformation. (If you and your spouse are dealing with very serious issues, such as alcoholism or abuse, however, I urge you to seek support from a counselor or pastor as you seek to work through these problems.)

Still don't think it's possible? It's really not much different than planning a fabulous vacation. Imagine sitting with your mate on the couch, reading about some far-off exotic land in the travel section of your Sunday paper. The photos tease you into feeling like you're almost there, surrounded by the sights and sounds of a tropical paradise.

Although reading about this enchanting land doesn't get you there, it can inspire you. Intoxicated with possibilities, you and your mate may start talking, dreaming, and planning. You decide right then and there you *will* travel to this destination on your next vacation. In your mind's eye you see the white sand on those tropical islands. You feel the fine linens on the plush bed in the seaside resort. You hear the rolling waves as you rock softly in a hammock beneath a palm tree. You can almost taste the fine seafood at a waterfront restaurant as you watch the sun set over the horizon. Ahhhhhh.

This vacation is possible, but it takes inspiration, perspiration, and lots of planning. As enchanting as a trip to a tropical island sounds, I want you to imagine another trip—the most incredible trip of a lifetime—a journey leading you to your soul mate. As with planning your dream vacation, this trip will also take preparation and commitment. For twelve weeks I want you to be intentional about finding your soul mate, meticulously following the planned route laid out in this book. Letting your imagination soar, trust that the map I give you will lead you to soft music, quiet interludes, and shared secrets with the one you love.

## Let the Music Play

Maybe it's been a long time since you had romantic feelings. The music has faded into the background and you no longer feel close enough—physically, emotionally, or spiritually—to dance in perfect rhythm with your mate. You have doubts that your ordinary, routine relationship can be transformed. I understand.

But, you *want* to dance again. While perhaps hidden, the romantic in you is still alive, buried beneath the busyness of daily life. You've learned to distract yourself so as not to be disappointed. But you want nothing more than for your mate to be your soul mate again.

Whether you've been married for forty-two years or engaged for four months, this kind of relating is possible. What is needed is a change of heart, a change of pace, and a change of mind. Moving from mate to soul mate is possible. All that stands between you and an enchanting relationship is a little inspiration.

This, again, is very good news. Like the physician listening to the patient list symptoms that fit into a predictable pattern, together we can learn the predictable problems that lead to a mundane marriage. Focusing on these problems, and then replacing them with "soul mate behavior," leads to incredible changes.

## Bringing Out the Best in Your Mate

Counselors, like doctors, are trained to focus on problems. We identify the patterns challenges take and then intervene. While this approach is helpful, it is not enough. Instead of focusing only on what is going wrong, we must focus on replacing problem behavior with constructive, healing behavior. In this book, we'll discuss ways you can interact with your mate so he or she responds with love, kindness, and affection, demonstrating that he or she is downright head over heels in love with you.

While this may initially sound too good to be true, positive action almost always leads to positive reaction. When you treat your mate with love and respect, you're likely to receive love and respect in return. When you intentionally choose to bring excitement and energy into your marriage, your mate is likely to respond in kind. You can, in large part, determine how your mate will respond to you.

In active pursuit of this "soul mate encounter," let's briefly consider some of the tools you'll master to revolutionize your relationship.

1. *Reevaluating your perspective.* As the Scriptures say, "Those who live only to satisfy their own sinful nature will harvest decay and death from that sinful nature. But those who

live to please the Spirit will harvest everlasting life from the Spirit" (Galatians 6:8, NLT). In other words, the choices you make have predictable effects. This is particularly true when it comes to deciding whether to view your spouse from a positive or negative perspective. Even during difficult times you can choose to amplify the positive.

2. *Choosing rose-colored glasses.* When you choose to focus on the positive in your spouse, you'll be happier, healthier, and able to relate more effectively. Learn when to focus on a problem and when to ignore it. Even if you're in a challenging marriage, you can learn how to build a bridge from a problem to the benefit inherent in it. Every crisis is an opportunity for positive change. Every frustrating issue in your relationship is an opportunity to explore character changes that need to be made.

3. *Bringing out the best qualities of your spouse.* Learn not only how to notice your mate's best qualities but how to amplify them and create an environment in which they can thrive.

4. *Remembering the reasons your mate loves you.* Your mate fell in love with some magical qualities in you. Are they still apparent? Do you remember why he or she fell in love with you, and are you nurturing those traits in yourself?

5. *Giving up distractions to the dream.* Calling forth your mate's best qualities takes focus. Give up distractions and practice recognizing, amplifying, and remembering these qualities again and again. You must notice, pay attention to, and attend to the qualities you want in your relationship.

6. *Embracing the ripple effect.* When you notice what's wonderful about your spouse and he or she notices what's great about you, good feelings ripple back and forth in the relationship. You have the power to begin this wave of positive feelings, positive behaviors, and positive attitudes. You have the power to change negative patterns into positive ones.

7. *Nurturing your mate's dreams.* Your mate has his or her own musings, ideas, and dreams. These hopes can be nurtured and encouraged; in fact, everything you do to actively encourage your mate's dreams will build intimacy.

8. *Teaching your mate to nurture your dreams.* When you nurture your spouse's dreams, he or she is more likely to nurture yours. And when you dream together, a powerful bond occurs.

9. *Preparing your best to meet your spouse's best.* Instead of perpetuating destructive patterns, agree not only to notice each other's best but also to nurture it and allow your best to be front and center as well.

10. *Unleashing the power of positive gossiping.* When you focus on the positive qualities of your mate, you naturally talk about him or her. Telling others about your spouse makes his or her positive qualities more real to you and creates an extremely favorable dynamic in the relationship.

11. *Initiating change by encouragement.* It's no secret—we make changes more easily and effectively with encouragement than with criticism. While encouragement breeds cooperation and trust, criticism breeds resentment and hostility. Learn to create an environment filled with positivity, warmth, and encouragement.

12. *Maintaining mutual admiration.* It takes intentionality and focus to maintain positive momentum. Resist the natural temptation to slip into negativity and regression, and insist on a mutually admiring relationship.

Positivity. Upwardly spiraling relationships. That is what this book is about. Determine to bring out the best in your mate, and encourage him or her to bring out the best in you. The result will be revolutionary.

While it takes effort to shift from the criticism and negativism that come naturally, you can do it. If you are intentional, you can choose a new perspective that will positively change your relationship.

You are facing the opportunity of a lifetime, a chance to discover your soul mate and be a soul mate. The change must begin with you, but I guarantee your mate can't help but respond favorably to these changes.

## Teaching a Chicken to Dance

Behavior is amazingly predictable. We are creatures of habit, and we dance in predictable ways. Not only that, but our mates react and respond in predictable ways as well. Action leads to reaction, and so on.

Before ending one of my last sessions with Susie and Dillon, I used a story to challenge them to maintain the changes in the way they related to one another.

"Did you know you can actually teach a chicken to dance?" I asked.

They looked puzzled, as couples always do when I start this story. I had their attention, however.

"It's true," I continued. "Ask any experimental psychologist who, for whatever reasons, studies these things. If you reinforce a chicken for making certain moves by giving it a small pellet of corn, it will make more and more moves toward your desired goal. Assuming you want to teach the chicken to dance, you reinforce every move that even resembles the dance you are teaching."

Susie and Dillon looked at each other, a slow grin breaking out on their faces. They were beginning to see the connection between chickens and people—specifically, them!

"Here is what else my colleagues discovered. If you kick the chicken in the head when it makes a move in an undesirable direction, it will flop over dead or run frantically for its life. Either way, the dance is over.

"So if you want to teach a chicken—or a spouse—to dance, you can. The choice is yours."

That is your task as well—to pay attention and carefully choose how you will behave with the one who means the most to you. As you prepare to begin implementing positive change over the next twelve weeks, begin by simply noticing what brings negativity to your relationship and what brings positivity and joy. Don't worry too much about changing anything for now. Just notice.

As Dillon and Susie discovered, you don't have to do what you've always done. It really is possible to change your focus, to notice what brings your relationship down and what takes it back up. You can master the art of discerning what makes your mate melt with desire to be near you. This book is all about making new choices as well as embracing and mastering new strategies. It's about hope and the belief that a "twinkle in your eyes" love is still possible, no matter how long you've been married. It's about catching each other making the right moves, and then building upon those actions.

At the end of every chapter, I'll offer a Weekly Quiz, giving you an opportunity to reflect on that week's lesson and apply it to your life. You'll quickly notice your strengths, as well as those areas needing further attention. The "Putting It into Practice" questions and exercises that follow each quiz provide practical tools you and your spouse can use to strengthen your marriage.

You won't always relate perfectly, of course, but if you can isolate the things you do that are hurtful and identify those that are helpful, it is possible to make choices so that your mate falls in love with you all over again.

You have an incredible opportunity, and it all begins with you. You can decide to draw closer to your spouse as his or her soul mate. This decision can make a profound difference, one that I'm privileged to enjoy with my wife, Christie. Singlehandedly you can begin the transformation process.

Are you ready to be in a marriage filled with zest and vitality, where your mate adores you and where you adore your mate? It's all very possible.

So let's get started.

# REEVALUATING YOUR PERSPECTIVE

*Blessed are those who have not seen and yet have believed.*
—John 20:29

## SIGNS THAT YOU NEED A NEW PERSPECTIVE

1. You're as surprised when someone compliments your spouse as you are when Simon Cowell has something nice to say about a contestant on *American Idol.*
2. You're more than willing to assign responsibility for your marital problems—to your spouse.
3. You think there's a better chance of winning the lottery (without buying a ticket) than there is for your marriage to become exciting again.
4. You include your prerogative to hold a grudge against your spouse on your personal list of "inalienable rights."
5. It bugs you when your spouse ruins a perfectly pleasant day by bringing up a problem or concern.

Not appearing a day over twenty-five, Dr. Taylor, my ophthalmologist, gave me a few more specifics about cataract surgery. Parts of the surgery would be unpleasant, and I was a bit anxious as I considered having my left lens replaced.

"I take it that your vision has been getting worse," Dr. Taylor said, making notes in my chart.

"For a while it was just an annoyance," I said, opening and closing each eye, "but it bothers me all the time now. I feel like I'm looking out through a dark, smudged lens."

"I can see why your world looks dark and blurry. It's like looking through a dirty window. We're going to put a new window into your eye, and you'll love the difference."

He reminded me that the risks to the surgery were very minor compared to the benefits. "Everyone has to decide for themselves when it's time for the cataract surgery. But if it were up to me, and I had the fuzziness you obviously have, I'd say do it now."

Glancing down at the numbers he'd calculated on my vision, Dr. Taylor enthusiastically told me, "You're not going to believe the difference."

"Perfect," I said, smiling. "Let's get it done."

I felt comfortable with Dr. Taylor. Though young, my doctor had a demeanor that gave me confidence in his skills.

I was prepared to undergo the procedure for another reason. Just two years ago I had cataract surgery on my right eye. I knew the routine.

My vision had gradually regressed into a lifeless and blurry picture as the first cataract grew. I didn't realize how bad it was until the doctor gave me visual examples of clear versus gray vision. "You get used to the way you view things and don't know there is a much better way," he said, going on to talk about the quick, relatively painless procedure of installing a new lens on the cornea of my eye.

After undergoing a half-hour preoperative anesthetic and a four-minute implant procedure, I went from having blurred vision of grays in my right eye to seeing clear, crisp images of reds, yellows, and blues. The difference was startlingly dramatic. I'm now a poster boy for cataract surgery, and soon I will have two eyes with clear, dynamic vision.

## Fuzzy Lens Relationships

I can't help comparing my literal blurry, cataract-laden lenses with the figurative dark-colored glasses so many of my clients wear. They often don't realize how their negative attitudes and interactions affect their relationship with their mates. Just as I lost out on the vibrancy of life because of blurry and dull vision, so many couples wearing dark-colored glasses forfeit a vibrant marital relationship due to their perspective on the situation.

One hurt here, a negative interaction there, and soon the relationship takes on a hazy, disappointing hue. Hardly aware that they're seeing their mate through a foggy lens, husbands and wives can begin to interact from a distorted perspective. This "fog," however, is far from innocuous—it taints and discolors everything a person sees when looking at his or her mate.

Laurie and Stephen came to see me when the lens in their relationship became a bit distorted. Walking toward them for our first meeting, I watched the couple chat with one another in my waiting room. They had arrived separately and appeared to be catching up with one another when I greeted them. I introduced myself and escorted them back to my office.

"Where should we sit?" Laurie asked nervously. "We've never done this before. We weren't sure if there'd be a couch or what," she said.

"Sorry to disappoint you," I said, smiling. "Just old-fashioned living room chairs."

Looking at each other, Laurie jumped in. "We're not sure where to start."

Stephen raised his eyebrows, indicating he wasn't sure how to start either.

"Stephen means the world to me," Laurie began. "But we've slipped a bit since we married five years ago. This is our second marriage, and we're not going to let this thing get away from us. Been there, done that."

"I think we've developed some small habits that we want to stop," added Stephen. "We've started seeing each other in a negative light and saying hurtful things to one another, and that is just not our heart.

"We know better than to do what we're doing, but I think both Laurie and I have become too complacent in the way we look at one another. We want to bring the magic back into our marriage. We think we need someone to hold us accountable for doing that.

"You go ahead and talk," Stephen said softly, turning to Laurie. Seeing her hesitate, he added, "It's okay if you talk about me. I know I've got some things to change."

"I'm not here to put Stephen down," Laurie said.

"Go for it," Stephen reiterated. "It's really okay. I want him to know what I do that takes us down. Of course, after that you can add some wonderful things about me too." He grinned.

"He really is all that," Laurie said, reaching for Stephen's hand.

"So, what's happened?" I asked. "Tell me about your marriage and the pluses and minuses."

"We had a wonderful marriage," she said slowly. "I don't know what's happened. We used to spend lots of time together, but now not so much. With the economy in trouble, I've gone back to nursing four nights a week, and Stephen has had to pick up the slack at work after a large company layoff.

"We used to share with each other how much we cared about the other, but not so often anymore." She shrugged. "Maybe we take our love for each other for granted now, but I think we both feel like we're losing something really important."

"In a sad way," Stephen stated, "we both feel a little like we're dying on the vine. Do you know what we mean?"

"Dying on the vine doesn't happen overnight," I said, a slight smile on my face. "It takes a fair amount of neglect to get a vine to die. So tell me what's happening—or not happening."

"We used to be close," Laurie added, "and now it seems like we're too busy for each other. We're both too rushed. If something funny happens at work, I always think, *I can't wait to tell Stephen!* But when I get home, I'm bone tired and Stephen is heading off to work, so it never happens. When he gets home in the afternoons, he often seems preoccupied. If he is behind at work, he gets critical with me for anything and everything. When he's irritable, I just back off."

"When I'm cranky, I get testy," admitted Stephen. "I start to think Laurie is making too many demands on me. I start to actually believe she doesn't love me. I know it sounds crazy, but that's one of the attitudes I can easily slip into."

"Me too," Laurie added. "When Stephen gets busy, I think maybe he doesn't love me as much anymore. I even get a little panicky."

"Then we reassure each other and pull things together," Stephen continued. "But we can't believe it's even gotten to the point where we question each other's love."

"You know, folks," I began, "I know you're very concerned about these patterns, and that encourages me. I'll bet you're already trying to change some of these patterns. Is that right?"

Both nodded.

Far from being overly concerned, I felt slightly encouraged. Laurie and Stephen were strongly committed to one another. They had enjoyed vibrancy early in their marriage, clearly appreciating each

................................................................................................

**HOPE IS CLOSE AT HAND**
Once you are prepared to accept responsibility for some of the negative patterns creeping into your marriage and replace them with healthier ones, you can begin to restore your marriage's vitality.

................................................................................................

other. If they were willing to follow my lead and follow biblical principles, they could find that vibrancy again. They were ready to take full responsibility for negative patterns creeping into their marriage, and they were willing to replace them with positive ones. We were off to a great start.

## Believing Is Seeing

Can you relate to Stephen and Laurie? Perhaps you had a dynamic marriage at one point, only to discover that you have begun allowing negative patterns to develop. It happens easily, often without notice.

I spent the first session helping Stephen and Laurie uncover the destructive patterns that were developing in their marriage. I asked them to set their judgments aside, as much as possible, and simply notice with me what they were doing.

Upon reflection, Stephen and Laurie agreed they had stopped sharing with each other personal stories from their day. Instead they tended to walk in the door and plop down on the couch, hardly sharing a word. No wonder their relationship began to shrivel and become mundane.

We are a pattern-seeking species. Not only do we have a tendency to slip into patterns of behavior—which was happening with Stephen and Laurie—but we tend to see situations in patterns. Something happens and we make a judgment about it. Something happens again and we make another judgment, leading to an opinion. Soon we've developed a judgment that is lasting, affecting our behavior.

We use this pattern-forming ability all the time. For example, how many times have you seen an image in a cloud? That image, of course, is not in the cloud—we have imposed our own interpretation on the way it's shaped. How often have you been sure you've spotted something you're looking for in the distance, only to find when you're up close that it is something totally different? Recently while out sailing and looking for whales, I spotted what I thought to be a sea lion more than once, only to find out it was a bobbing piece of driftwood. So much for perception.

Though we may not realize it, we bring this same pattern-forming tendency to our relationships. The evening meal is the most natural time of the workday for Laurie and Stephen to talk. He arrives home shortly before dinner, and Laurie leaves for her job a few hours later. A few weeks after the layoffs, Laurie began noticing that Stephen often came home from work looking tired and anxious. Laurie asked him several times when she thought his boss would get Stephen some help. She intended her query to show her concern; however, he bristled inside at the implication that he wasn't capable of keeping up with his workload. More than once, he snapped at Laurie, leading her to conclude that it wasn't safe to probe too deeply. They never discussed their perceptions; instead, they both learned to steer clear of anything other than small talk over dinner.

Unfortunately, when it comes to relationships, once we've made a decision about how something appears, it is difficult to change our minds. Once we've made a judgment about a person or viewed an event from a certain perspective, it's a difficult and arduous task to view it from another angle.

......................................................................

**BELIEVING IS SEEING**
What you believe to be true about your spouse
will affect how you view him or her.

......................................................................

Our pattern-forming abilities are acute and fairly accurate at times, while completely flawed at other times. Consider how quickly you form an opinion about whether or not you like someone. Consider how long it takes to change your mind if you first decide you don't like that person.

Let's apply this same principle to the issue at hand—viewing your mate through dark-colored glasses. We each develop attitudes toward our mates, and these attitudes fluctuate over time. Depending on what we believe, we will "see" different things in them.

If, for example, we believe we are loved and cherished, we're likely to respond positively toward our mates. If, on the other hand, we feel disrespected, we're going to have difficulty acting with love toward them. Can you see that our attitudes—what we believe—are critical to how we behave?

Stephen and Laurie came to see me because they were developing some troubling behavior patterns, which were affecting their attitudes toward one another as well. Each began to question whether the other really held him or her in positive regard. Each started to wonder if he or she was really loved. With this attitude, their marriage lost its stable footing, further darkening their relational lens.

A profound truth and central principle of this book is simply this: believing is seeing. What you believe to be true about your mate will influence how you view him or her. Your attitudes will influence how you treat your spouse. In everything, your attitude is showing.

## Looking at Your Attitude

Your attitude is the lens through which you view your mate, seeing him or her either in a primarily positive or predominantly negative light. Have you considered your attitude toward your mate?

It is time to step back and evaluate your perspective. Are you wearing brightly colored glasses, allowing light and goodness in, or are you wearing dark-colored glasses, focusing on all that is wrong in your relationship? Your answers to the following questions will help you determine your attitude.

1. Do you believe your mate loves you?
2. Do you believe your mate has your best interests in mind?
3. Do you believe he or she sincerely cares about your well-being?
4. Do you notice more of your mate's positive or negative qualities?

5. Do you dwell more on your mate's positive qualities or negative ones?
6. Do you spend time encouraging your mate's positive qualities?
7. Do you pray for your mate?
8. What single word best describes your attitude toward your mate?

Once you've answered these questions, consider what you've learned. Did you decide your mate truly does love you and has your best interests in mind? Do you believe he or she cares about you and your well-being? Is your attitude generally positive or negative, trusting or distrusting, hopeful or discouraged? Your answers reveal how you view your mate and your relationship with him or her—not necessarily the reality of the situation.

If you're unsure how your spouse really feels, check out your perceptions with him or her. Find out if what you believe to be true is actually the case. This is an opportunity to clarify misperceptions. Your answers will direct you to some important discussions you need to have. Next reflect on how your attitude influences your interactions with your mate.

I often tell my clients that perception is everything. What you believe to be real, in many instances, becomes your reality. If you perceive your mate to be against you, you will likely take on an adversarial position against him or her. If, on the other hand, you perceive your spouse as being primarily *for* you, you will likely have a positive attitude toward him or her.

Now here's where things get interesting. While perception is everything, perception is not necessarily accurate. Let me give you a practical example from my life.

Recently our grown children visited for the weekend. Excited to see one another and wanting to spend lots of time catching up, we all stayed up well past my bedtime. Around eleven o'clock I politely excused myself and went to bed. I quickly fell asleep, only to wake an hour later to laughing. I immediately became annoyed. I tried, unsuccessfully, to muffle the noise, but in my sleepy state I became increasingly irritated. When my wife finally came to bed, I had been nursing a grudge for over an hour and made some sharp comments.

In that moment I viewed my wife as uncaring, insensitive, and unloving—traits completely uncharacteristic of her. My perception had been appreciably altered by my tiredness, lack of assertiveness, and ability to hold a grudge.

After a restless night's sleep and a few more terse words, I finally apologized and began to review the situation. The truth of the matter is our children were having a good time and deserved to have fun with their mother. The truth of the matter is that the children were not being insensitive. In fact, they had tried to be quiet and sensitive to my feelings. The truth of the matter is that I didn't get up and ask them to keep the noise down, or join in the fun, or find a good book to read. Instead, I allowed myself to fall headlong into a pit of self-pity—and a terribly foul mood.

Can you see the difference perception makes? Yes, I missed out by not recognizing my error sooner. But what if I had been a bit more cantankerous, deciding to hold my position in spite of evidence to the contrary? What if I had dug in my heels, rehearsing the "rightness" of my position? Christie and I could have become divided, our hearts set against one another. The results could have been disastrous.

## Moods—Temporary Insanity

While I escaped that evening with just a few hours of tension, things could have been worse. Moods can envelop us, causing us to lose perspective. A little anger, a dose of discouragement, some nursed resentment, and soon our thoughts can spin out of control.

Not long ago I received a call from a woman who is incredibly anxious. Her marriage is slipping away, and her husband of fifteen years is seriously considering a separation.

I've worked with Gayle and her husband, Michael, for some time. Unfortunately, they came to me late in the game, only after years of conflict. Now Michael is tired and restless, saying he no longer has the strength to continue fighting.

Michael's mood is one of profound discouragement. He projects past disappointments into the future, creating a perception of despair. He cannot see how things will possibly get better since the past several years have been so bad. Gayle is intensely fearful, and she wonders how she can survive if her husband leaves. Both feel desperate.

Their moods are palpable. Talking with Gayle on the phone was stressful for me, as I felt powerless to save this couple.

"You've got to do something," Gayle protested. "You've got to make Michael see that he's making a huge mistake. God can save our marriage. Michael just needs to give us more time."

I felt sorry for Gayle. If only I could offer her the assurance that Michael wouldn't leave. What I did was try to help her see that clutching at Michael, trying to use guilt to induce him into staying, was not the answer. She might have to let him go, if that was his intent, and then begin working on their marriage in a new and different way.

In other words, she could decide to end their negative, vicious cycles by refusing to beg and plead with him to stay. As frightening as that was for her, she understood that refusing to get locked into her part of the cycle could instill a small dose of hope that things could change. We could then begin to unlock other destructive patterns in their marriage, working to build a spiral of positivity. As we talked, Gayle finally began to see that criticizing Michael would do no good and that viewing him continuously in a negative light only reinforced her resentment.

Michael revealed his troubled state in a counseling session not long after.

"I don't have any hope," he said. "I hate the idea of leaving Gayle and the kids, but all we do is fight. That's all we're ever going to do."

"I can understand your discouragement, Michael," I offered, "but the past doesn't have to dictate the future. Just because you two have fought a lot in the past doesn't mean you can't learn new skills."

"I don't believe anything can change," he said, looking down. His mood was dark, his face hollow from continued disappointment.

"You feel hopeless," I said, "and that colors everything you see. But you and Gayle can learn new skills. She is motivated to change and that is a good sign. You both can make a decision to change old patterns—you can decide to rebuild, interact in healthier ways, and solve your old problems. The work is very doable if you're willing to give it a try. One step at a time, Michael."

Michael looked up, taking in every word.

"I'll think about it," he said cautiously. "But I'm not promising anything."

At this writing Michael and Gayle have begun pulling out of their negative spin. Though cautious and still somewhat discouraged, Michael is starting to see Gayle in a different light. He notices her efforts to be sensitive to his needs and less clingy. Gayle notices the slight shift in Michael's attitude and behavior and is mildly encouraged. A new light is creeping into their marriage.

## Many Angles

While perception helps us frame our experience, it's often very inaccurate. Moods tend to make us intractable, closed to new information. Michael's perceptions had become rigid, not allowing new, helpful information to become part of the equation. He didn't even notice the first few times Gayle didn't panic when he threatened to leave. Only slowly and with the help of counseling did he realize that his wife was not the needy, emotional woman he had come to view her as.

**CHOOSE YOUR PERSPECTIVE**
By remaining flexible and willing to see things from different points of view, you can begin to stop viewing your spouse negatively.

So how can Michael and Gayle's situation help you? Realize that there are many ways of viewing the same event. You don't have to view any event or set of circumstances from a reduced, narrow perspective. You can cultivate an open mind and an open heart, embracing new possibilities.

If ten people view the same event and then are interviewed about it, you'll get ten different interpretations and observations. Things are not always as they seem.

Let's revisit the night when our children kept me awake. Consider what would have happened if, when their laughing woke me up, I had thought:

- *It's great that our children are having such fun.*
- *We're so fortunate that our children love being with us.*

- *How wonderful that our children enjoy each other.*
- *Here is an opportunity for me to kick up my heels.*
- *Our children would welcome my participation.*

Each of these statements, by the way, was true. Sadly, I couldn't see them at the time because I was wearing dark-colored glasses. My wife, wearing rose-colored glasses, had a ball. Guess who got the better deal?

When it comes to relating to your mate, you have a great deal of room to decide how you will view things. The key is flexibility and openness to seeing things from different angles. Healthy couples stay loose, looking at things from different points of view. In fact, they practice seeing situations from different angles, asking their mates for input into other possible points of view and empathizing with their positions. They turn things over in their minds, listen to alternate perspectives, and remain open to new information.

## Attitudes Are Contagious

Recently I was grousing about the amount of rainfall in Washington State to a woman who is originally from Kansas.

"I absolutely love the green of Washington," she said, "and it's our rainfall that makes it so beautiful."

"Yeah," I continued, "but we get too much of it."

She couldn't believe her ears. "Well," she said, "I absolutely love the moist, soft air. I love the damp breeze coming off the salt water. I love the green mountains and forests, the lakes, streams, and ocean. I think you're taking for granted all that you have here." Her enthusiastic words stopped me in my tracks, reminding me that we have the opportunity of viewing things from different angles.

In his groundbreaking book *Emotional Intelligence*, Daniel Goleman explains that we actually "transmit and catch moods from each other." That means some exchanges are toxic, some are nourishing. "This emotional exchange," he says, "is typically at a subtle, almost imperceptible level; the way a salesperson says thank you can leave us feeling ignored, resented, or genuinely welcomed and appreciated. We catch feelings from one another as though they were some kind of social virus."[1]

So that's why I get cranky when my wife is in a bad mood! And that explains why she gets irritable when I'm moping around the house! This also explains why I'm on top of the world when Christie greets me at the door and says, "Hello, handsome. I'm glad you're home." After a long day, a warm hug and a sweet word make everything right with the world.

Goleman is, in my experience, right on.

I recall when our younger son, Tyson, was an adolescent and prone to grumbling. When things in his world were not suiting him, he had a way of letting everyone—and I mean everyone!—know it. His attitude could be seen and felt from some distance.

For a time, Tyson would come to the dinner table in a bad mood and expect us to ignore him.

"Just leave me alone," he would say. "You don't have to let my bad mood affect you. It's my problem, and I'll get over it on my own."

"That's not the way it works, Ty," we'd reply. "Your mood affects the whole family."

"Well, it shouldn't," he protested. "Don't let it bother you."

"That's easier said than done," we'd say. "Moods are contagious. We feel what you're feeling. We're happy to try to help you if you want to talk about a problem, but if you're simply going to be grumpy, you're going to have to deal with it on your own."

That's exactly what we decided—he could go to his room and linger in his bad mood as long as he wanted, but he wasn't allowed to come to the dinner table and pull down the mood of the entire family with him.

Our attitudes, whether good or bad, are contagious. The good news, as we will discuss in greater detail later, is that we have the power to influence the attitudes of our mates by our attitudes. We can allow our bad moods to resonate back and forth between us, or we can choose to influence each other with our positive moods and attitude.

## Bringing Out the Worst in Each Other

Dark moods cast a pall over the happiest moment, the most peaceful home. They create an environment of confusion, leaving everyone feeling helpless and perplexed as to how to eliminate the heavy mood.

While all bad moods are troubling, some moods cause more damage than others. Some are particularly hurtful and can move your marriage from a place of safety and satisfaction to a place of hardship. Here are a few attitudes I want you to be especially careful to guard against. These attitudes cannot be allowed free rein if you want to create an environment where love can grow.

*Things are hopeless.* Nothing pulls down a relational mood faster than hopelessness. When Michael insisted to Gayle that there was no hope for changing their marriage, his despair was contagious, leading her to give up hope as well. A dark mood creates a cloud of gloom over a marriage, creating a sense of hopelessness and sometimes profound discouragement.

Fortunately, the situation is rarely as bleak as the dark mood might indicate. There is almost always a crack or crevice for hope to seep through, and the smallest amount of hope is enough to change an attitude. As people of faith we can ask for the wisdom of God to help us find answers where we feel discouraged.

*You don't care about me.* When antagonistic feelings are swirling inside us like a bad case of stomach flu, it's hard to have warm and fuzzy feelings for our mates. Perhaps we've been nursing these bad feelings for some time, leaving little room for positive feelings. If so, we're sure to develop a foul attitude.

But the truth of the matter is usually (and hopefully!) that we do care for our mates. And they care about us. Perhaps the caring has been shielded by bad attitudes and discouraging behavior, but we're one small step from turning everything around. One small act of caring leads to another and another and another. And over time, caring actions lead to a new attitude being formed within us.

*I have a right to be angry.* Oh, the delight of righteous indignation! We spend so much time rehearsing how right we are and how wrong our mates are. We spin things easily in our direction, so our mates are the "bad guys" and we're the innocent parties. We're the victims and they're the villains. This attitude is dangerous, damaging, and incredibly divisive.

But what if your spouse has deeply wounded you through some sort of betrayal? Of course you'll feel hurt and anger. The truth of the matter, though, is that we never have the right to camp out with our anger. While you may have been victimized, setting up an angry house will do no good. Allow yourself to feel anger, and then move into effective action. Make choices. Set boundaries. Reframe the problem so that you're working on solutions. Accept that your mate is very human, just like you.

*There's a right and wrong way of doing things.* Once we believe we are doing things the "right" way and our mates are doing them the "wrong" way, we shift into a disgruntled and angry attitude. This narrow perspective, limiting our vision, only serves to alienate our mates from us.

Remember Laurie, who fretted that her husband's work demanded too much of him? Concerned that Stephen's supervisor was taking advantage of her husband, she repeatedly asked when his boss would ease his workload. Once the couple finally discussed the situation, Stephen told Laurie that his boss's responsibilities had also increased. Stephen had begun giving his boss weekly updates and getting clarification on which projects were most pressing. His approach enabled him to feel less overwhelmed during an otherwise stressful work situation.

Most often, when we loosen up and take a breath, we realize how wrong we've been to look at things from such a narrow point of view. Practicing viewing issues from multiple angles allows us to see our mates with new eyes—not as adversaries, but as beloved spouses.

*My spouse is against me.* When we assume our mates are opposing us, it's easy to view them as the enemy. *Why won't he see things my way? Why won't she go along with my plan?* As we rehearse these negative beliefs, our anger and bitterness grow, and we push further away from one another. With enough rehearsing, we can actually view our spouses as being overly critical toward us. That's exactly what Stephen did.

Of course, this perspective may be wrong. Our mates can disagree with us without being "against us." When we see with new eyes that they love us in spite of disagreeing with us, we soften and are willing to draw them closer.

The first step to revitalizing your marriage is reevaluating your perspective. By now I hope you have considered the possibility that your negative attitude, internally rehearsed and justified, may actually be causing serious harm to your marriage. This first week's challenge is to responsibly inspect your attitude, considering the distinct possibility that there are better ways to view your situation.

It is tempting to slip into passivity, believing you have little impact on what happens in your marriage. Nothing could be further from the truth. Yes, you can simply react to situations, but there is a better way. You can act deliberately, choosing those actions and words that will bring out the best in your mate. Obviously, you will benefit tremendously from the more positive approach.

Now that you've taken off your dark-colored glasses, what's next? In chapter 2, we'll explore how you can put on rose-colored ones. Instead of dreading conflict in your marriage, learn to see the possibilities as you work through struggles between you and your spouse. Instead of seeing all that is wrong with your mate, consider viewing him or her with new eyes. Looking for the positive qualities in your marriage and in your mate will lead to a stronger, closer partnership.

## Weekly Quiz

It's time to evaluate your marital perspective. Remember that positive actions almost always lead to positive reactions. And positive actions are easier if you start from a positive perspective. You have the ability to set the tone for your relationship. Consider how you would act in the following scenario:

You sent your spouse to the store an hour ago, asking him to buy just eggs, milk, and dog food. You thought he'd be home by now, and your dog, who's now barking and pacing the floor, is even more keyed up than you. You think to yourself:

a) *Figures. I knew I should have gone to the store myself. That man can never find anything! Hmmm. I bet he's stalling so he can get out of doing the dishes.*

b) *I'm so glad he went out for me. I knew it might be hard to find the brand of dog food that Brutus likes. I wouldn't be surprised if he's had to go to another store to locate it.*

........................................................................................

## PUTTING IT INTO PRACTICE THIS WEEK

1. Take some time to talk with your mate about the "lens" through which you see and respond to one another. For help, refer back to the questions on pages 7–8.

2. Recall an incident that led to an argument or misunderstanding between the two of you. Allow each other to give your perspective on the situation. Then discuss the differences in your perceptions and whether both might have at least some validity.

3. Look over the list of "toxic" attitudes on pages 14–15. Which, if any, do you think exist between the two of you?

*Week 2*

# CHOOSING
# ROSE-COLORED GLASSES

*The optimist looks at the world through rose-tinted spectacles.*
—English proverb

**SIGNS THAT YOU NEED TO PUT ON ROSE-COLORED GLASSES**
1. You'd describe yourself as an emotional chicken rather than an emotional champion.
2. You try to duck out of sight when your spouse calls, "Honey, we need to talk."
3. You won't let your spouse forget the time he or she forgot your mom's birthday—three years ago.
4. The last time you sat down to for a heart-to-heart talk with your spouse was when you were debating whether to eat at McDonald's or Wendy's.
5. You'd rate your marriage as average—or worse—but are content to let it coast.

An old joke, popularized by President Reagan, goes something like this:

A very optimistic young boy happened upon a huge pile of horse manure and began shoveling excitedly. When someone asked him why he was digging in the manure, the boy answered enthusiastically, "With all this manure, there must be a pony in here somewhere!"

We laugh at the absurdity of this joke, yet some people really do see obstacles as opportunities, viewing challenges as times of growth. They welcome a downturn in the real estate market, realizing the possibilities of finding an underpriced home for sale. They turn the loss of a job into an opportunity to pursue that degree they never finished or to seek employment in a field they've only dreamt about.

If we can remain calm and get beyond the fear of the moment, we often will see opportunity hidden in the apparent calamity. We have a choice to put on either dark-colored glasses or rose-colored ones.

Just the other day my wife and I were caught in a sudden downpour in Seattle. As I began to grumble about the weather and feeling cold and damp, she did what she knows how to do best—she made a bridge from what I saw only as a problem to what she saw as a positive outcome.

"Seems like a perfect opportunity to head to your favorite coffee shop on Cherry Street and get a bowl of soup and a latte," she said, smiling.

Initially I was stuck wearing my dark-colored glasses. "Let's just go home and get dry," I said, ignoring her good humor.

"Oh, come on," she persisted. "We could slip over to Ivar's for a cup of chowder. It's right on the water."

With a bit of struggle, I mentally reached for my rose-colored glasses, pried off my dark-colored ones, and embraced the opportunity to indulge in an enjoyable time with my wife. I grabbed Christie's hand and headed for Cherry Street, with visions of sipping a rich latte and enjoying the art on the coffee shop's walls swirling in my head. And I smiled.

This is a simple example, perhaps, but the same principle applies no matter how big the problem seems. Whether you believe you can

........................................................................................

**YOU'RE ALWAYS RIGHT**
Whether you believe you can overcome adversity in your marriage or you can't, you're right. Choose to see each difficulty as an opportunity for growth.

........................................................................................

overcome any adversity in your marriage or you don't believe you can, you're right. Now that you've examined your perceptions in week 1, this week's task will be to embrace your ability and responsibility to adjust your attitude, refusing simply to cope with a mediocre marriage and looking for opportunities to increase the exhilaration and excitement instead. Quite simply, doing so is your choice.

Believe me, there will be trials in your marriage either way. If you choose to wear dark-colored glasses, you'll see only darkness. When looking only at the negatives, you'll notice everything your mate does wrong, and with a bit of rehearsal, you'll amplify his or her imperfections. Soon these imperfections will grate on you like the sounds of a screechy violin, and you'll likely bolt for the door.

If, on the other hand, you choose to see each difficulty as an opportunity for growth, a chance to grow and expand, your marriage can be filled with excitement. If you look for the pony buried in the manure or the coffee shop in the midst of the rainstorm, you'll end up with something wonderful.

## A Place to Grow Up

Have you heard this corny joke before? You come into marriage sure you've found your ideal, only to slip into an ordeal and then head out the door for a new deal. Sadly, this isn't far from the truth for some couples. Faced head-on with problems that feel insurmountable, many couples see few options other than accepting a stagnant relationship or getting out altogether.

There is another way. There is a better way. The apostle James put it like this: "When troubles come your way, consider it an opportunity for great joy. For you know that when your faith is tested, your endurance has a chance to grow. So let it grow, for when your endurance is fully developed, you will be perfect and complete, needing nothing" (James 1:2-4, NLT).

Pure joy? Who is he kidding? Is it possible that God knew our marriages would be places of testing and yet opportunities for growth? Yes! He knows that marriage is an excellent place to hone your relationship skills, face your weaknesses, and grow beyond them. He knew what he was doing when he instituted marriage—and that pure joy could be part of the equation.

Adversity can take an adequate marriage and transform it into a soul-mate marriage. Adversity has a way of either dividing or uniting us. We either pull together or push apart. During tough times, we see our mates either as our allies or our adversaries.

Now remember, attitude is everything. The lens through which you look will determine what you see. If you decide you made a monstrous mistake and that your marriage should be a lot easier, you're in for trouble. If you decide, however, that you will embrace challenges as a helpful path to move from mate to soul mate, you're going to feel a lot better.

Take a moment and consider the tough times in your marriage. This will take a few minutes and is best done with a piece of paper and a reflective attitude—keep those rose-colored glasses close.

Once you've got a cup of coffee in hand and your trusted journal sitting in front of you, consider the rough spots in your marriage. Zero in on a particular difficulty that you've moved beyond. How did you do it? How did you get beyond your irritation, frustration, and anger? I suspect you "leaned in" and faced the issue, deciding to overcome it, and then you did! Simply put, you reframed your experience. No longer did you view it as an insurmountable problem but as a bridge to better communication or a better way of living.

Maybe you came through a season of conflict that ended with a pact to lessen the contention and live in harmony. Perhaps you made a decision not to neglect your marriage any longer, just like Stephen and Laurie in chapter 1, whose marriage was never in jeopardy but had slipped into mediocrity. You became intentional about adding zest and vitality to your marriage. You watched your relationship begin to blossom and grow.

Whether you're in a mediocre marriage and want to make it better or you're in a good marriage and want to make it great, I can promise you this: There is no better place to grow than in your marriage. This is the time and here is the place for growth. The answers are not "out there" but in here, right where you are!

It's true. Rather than being a place to struggle and cope, your marriage offers opportunities like no other to practice new skills. Consider the abilities I'm developing in my marriage:

- Speaking the truth in love: I'm learning how to be assertive, respecting Christie's point of view while also sharing my own.
- Holding my tongue: I'm learning to choose the right time to share my feelings and desires.

- Speaking words of encouragement: I'm learning to step outside myself, watching for opportunities to meet Christie's need for encouragement.
- Managing my anger: I'm learning to voice anger in healthy rather than hurtful ways.
- Being vulnerable and intimate: I'm learning to risk coming close and allowing myself to be seen for who I am.

If it were not for my marriage, I am sure I would not have grown in the ways I have. Sure, I would have had it much easier if I had never been forced to make these changes. However, I'm convinced my life would be much less rich as well.

In *Transitions*, a favorite book of mine, William Bridges explains that life is not a straight line of shortest distances, but rather "life fish-

### NO BETTER PLACE TO GROW
Nowhere will you have more opportunities to learn to speak the truth in love, hold your tongue, manage your anger, or be vulnerable than in marriage.

tails its way across an undulating landscape. If you want to live, you need to give yourself over to the way of transition—to let go when life presents you with a time of ending, to abandon yourself to the neutral zone when that is where you find yourself, to seize the opportunity to make a new beginning when that moment presents itself."[1]

## Not a Bad Thing

My wife, Christie, looked over at me recently while lying in bed and said she needed to talk to me about something. I immediately felt tense, taking her simple statement as a warning that something unpleasant was to come. It was.

"We're settling into a ho-hum relationship, and I don't like it," she said. "You're starting to work too much, and we haven't gotten away in months."

I looked at her, unprepared for her criticism. I handled the situation poorly. I immediately became defensive and challenged her on her perception.

"How can you say that?" I said incredulously. "We went on vacation two months ago and had a great time. Yes, I've been working a lot lately, but you knew I'd have to put my nose to the grindstone once we got back."

"You don't have to be so defensive," she countered, bristling. "I just miss the great evenings we had together, and I want them back. I don't want you working into the evening or making professional phone calls after dinner. I want the magic back in our marriage."

I still couldn't believe Christie's criticisms. I worked hard to be a loving, tender husband. But I also had a thriving private practice and an active writing career. I wanted a great marriage and felt I could fit it into the open spaces of our lives. She wanted more.

After pouting for a few moments, I considered what she was saying. In effect, I chose to remove my dark-colored glasses and put on the rose-colored ones I keep on my bed stand for times such as these.

Doing so forced me to look at the situation in a new way. What was the opportunity in this encounter? How could I turn a potential fight into a challenging opportunity for growth? It would take a great deal of willpower and a shift in attitude, but I was up for the challenge.

"Okay," I said reluctantly. "How can I adjust things so you will be excited about us again? I want a magical marriage too, so I'm in."

With that she smiled, reaching over and grabbing my hand.

"I was thinking we might get away to a bed-and-breakfast this weekend. There are a couple of places in Port Townsend I've heard about. Maybe you could write all day Friday and then we could zip out Friday and Saturday night. We could try out that new Italian restaurant on the way up. Just you and me, babe. What do you say?"

"Deal," I said, smiling.

I lay in bed for a few more minutes, excited at how we had not only averted a conflict but had created an exciting date. It was a win-win proposition. Christie allowed me some room to write, and I created space for her so she could have my undivided attention. Not only was her confrontation not a bad thing, it was an incredible opportunity for us. All it took was taking off my dark-colored glasses and putting on my rose-colored ones.

## Feeling Good All Over

It is incredibly empowering to view a challenge not as a bad or even neutral thing but as something good. Once you do, you're no longer a victim of unfortunate circumstances; you're now in control. You no longer use your energies to avoid difficult situations but trust your abilities to face them and deal with them effectively.

This attitude, however, takes cultivation. You must develop skills of focus and intentionality. Pollyannaish, you say? No, what is needed is a readiness to transform every challenge into a positive outcome.

What if when Christie had mentioned her disappointment I had directed all my energies into defending myself and arguing with

**TAKE CONTROL**
Viewing a problem positively will put you back in control and help you find the opportunity in what you had viewed as a negative.

her? Perhaps I would have "won" the argument, but only at great cost. I certainly would have gotten the conflict I dreaded, and more than likely Christie would have bottled future hurts and longings inside.

Because I chose an approach that didn't come as naturally, Christie and I arrived at a much better result. You can imagine my delight when one moment I was afraid of conflict and the next I was preparing for a fabulous weekend away with my wife. Can you imagine my shift from defensiveness and readiness for conflict to happiness and readiness for romance? Thanks to Christie's honesty and goodwill, we'd be staying at a wonderful bed-and-breakfast and most important, I'd be enjoying time with the woman who delights in me.

Can you feel the shift within Christie? One moment she was frightened of how this encounter would work out; the next she was feeling exuberant about the possibilities for our relationship. One moment she feared I would become defensive (as I first did) and refuse to listen to her, while the next she delighted in my openness and desire to please her.

In both cases, the first mind-set involved fear and doubt, while the other involved potential and excitement. The first left us feeling discouraged and frightened; the other allowed us to feel on top of the world, assured anything is possible. The choice was ours.

The most important shift, however, is the one that takes us from viewing ourselves as simply mates to seeing each other as soul mates. Had Christie allowed herself to settle into living with the way things were—which is tempting to do—we would have lost the opportunity to reach for more, to become soul mates. Had she been too frightened to reach out to me to ask for more, she and I would have slumped into mediocrity. We would have lived as mates, not soul mates.

Christie and I are learning what you can learn: one reaction leads to a similar reaction in the other. An aggressive response often leads to a counter-aggressive reaction. A sympathetic, soft response often creates the opportunity for a soft reaction. When I am open and ready to resolve issues, so is she. When I reach for new, creative ways of relating, she does as well. When I ask for more in our marriage, she is quick to give it. When she asks for more from me, I respond to her requests.

## No Settling

Once we settle for the way things are, we stop growing. Since everything is always in a state of decay and disintegration, a concept known in physics as *entropy*, we can never allow ourselves the luxury of going along with the status quo or being okay with what is. We must always reach for more. And more is always available to us. The moment we begin ignoring this truth, our marriages begin to deteriorate.

These are harsh words, but true. The truth is that we can predict marriages that will die long before the funeral. Many men and women want to be the bridegroom or bride, but don't want to be the husband or wife. Why? Because they don't want the daily drudgeries of marriage. And who can blame them? Who wants to settle into a life of diapers, dishes, detergent, and disinfectants? We want cuddles, kisses, and candlelight. There's nothing wrong with those desires; in fact, the very moment we give them up and settle for the mundane, our hope begins to die.

We must fight to find the ideal, even in the midst of those dirty diapers and dirty dishes. You may be pragmatic and insist that once the honeymoon ends all that's left is work, work, work. But I'm not buying it. I insist that we must never settle. We must never give up our dreams of being Prince Charming and Cinderella. And these dreams are possible if we hold on to those rose-colored glasses and insist on more from our marriages.

## Bearer of Good News

Every time Christie comes to me with a concern, I have a split second to decide if I want to hug or hurt the messenger. Of course I never want to hear bad news. I never want to hear complaints.

But I've made a most remarkable observation: If I receive her concerns with defensiveness, she feels unsafe and her concerns are likely to go underground, where they fester. If I respond to her message with disinterest or detachment, she feels belittled and insignificant, and she will likely push away from me.

If, on the other hand, I view her as a messenger of good news, inviting her concerns, criticisms, and complaints with receptivity, she will share them with me and we can seek out an agreeable solution. We can work together to make sure we both feel listened to, understood, and validated, and we can get on with the task of securing a solution that feels good to both of us.

Now I must be honest—I'm not always on top of my game. Sometimes I forget to greet the messenger with enthusiasm. I don't want to hear bad news, complaints, or personal failings. I realize, however, that each and every time I fail to greet the messenger, things turn out worse than if I had embraced her.

Trust me on this—I've tried it both ways. I've tried making it hard on her to come to me with concerns; this has never stopped the concern or dismissed the issue. I've also tried making her feel safe and secure, validating her concerns; this always works better. Our relationship has always been improved by facing problems and solving them and is never made better by avoiding problems.

One of the most powerful tools in this difficult endeavor is assuming Christie always has my well-being in mind, that her message to me is always one of ultimate good news. I assume she comes to me for the purpose of making our marriage even better than it already is. I believe in her goodwill toward me. With that assumption firmly in place, I listen to her concerns with a positive mind-set.

This approach is still largely counterintuitive, and thus difficult. It is perfectly natural to turn away from pain. We avoid doctors, dentists, income tax accountants, and attorneys. We want our problems to mysteriously evaporate into the night. But they don't, and we suffer the consequences.

So instead of thinking of problems and problem messengers in a negative light, play around with embracing problems. Hold them in your mind, turning them over a time or two and inspecting them from different points of view. Consider seeing the messenger, your mate, as someone intent on your well-being. Practice viewing him or her as the bearer of good news, someone who wants the best for you and your marriage—not as an evildoer intent upon your harm. Consider his or her messages as gifts.

## Overcoming Obstacles

Every challenge in life is a moment of possibility, a chance to grow and move forward, stronger than ever. How we face and embrace the challenge is everything, and our attitude determines the outcome.

Donald Clarke, in his book *A Marriage After God's Own Heart*, shares his thoughts on the matter.

> *The path to every significant achievement in life is full of roadblocks. Think of all the valuable, prized goals you have reached in your life: a college diploma, a graduate degree, building a business, getting a promotion, giving birth, raising a healthy family, buying a new home, growing spiritually, beating an addiction. . . . Remember how hard you had to work to get*

*to the finish line? Remember the obstacles, both internal and external, that you had to get past before you could claim victory? It's probably true that the more important the goal was, the more obstacles you encountered.*[2]

There are innumerable obstacles in moving from mate to soul mate. Each, however, is also an opportunity. Each is a chance to move you closer to being soul mates. Here are some steps necessary to viewing your mate through rose-colored glasses:

*Create a vision of a soul mate.* As obvious as this sounds, many people don't have a clue as to what a soul mate looks like. We are all too familiar with seeing people through the eyes of mediocrity. How about seeing your mate as someone capable of being fun, filled with enthusiasm and excitement? How about imagining your mate as someone who cares about you, who wants to know what you think and feel? View your mate as someone willing to converse with you, sharing intimate and transparent thoughts and feelings.

Armed with a vision of a soul mate, you pursue this profound level of intimacy. You settle for nothing less than being transparent and vulnerable, laughing easily, creating an atmosphere where you respect your mate and your mate respects you. You dedicate yourself to sharing dreams and encouraging your mate to dream and move steadfastly toward those dreams. You anticipate your mate's needs, and he or she anticipates yours. You share secret smiles and warm glances, and you light up when you encounter each other.

*Create space and time for being a soul mate.* In today's busy world, being a soul mate doesn't just happen. In addition to being intentional and having a vision, you must create time and space for being a soul mate. You must put other desires behind the importance of being a soul mate. You must purposefully plan activities and engagements where intimacy can thrive. Every time you greet your mate is a chance to create soul-mate relationship. Every conversation is an opportunity to show undivided attention and appreciation. Busyness and preoccupation cannot exist alongside creating space for a soul mate.

*Treasure your mate.* Were you to view your mate through rose-colored glasses, you couldn't help but treasure him or her. Imagine the following scenario:

Leaving the stress of the workday behind and having put on my rose-colored glasses, I pull in the driveway at night. I'm mindful of the importance of the first few minutes that my wife and I greet each other. Waltzing through the door in anticipation of meeting the most beautiful person on earth, I share my excitement.

"Good evening, dear," I say with enthusiasm. "It's great to see you. How was your day?" I grab my wife's hand and look deep into her eyes.

"Well," she says, "I had some highs and some lows."

"Yes," I respond, "and I'd like to hear about each one of them. Let's sit down and talk about our day." With that we walk to the couch and listen to each other share.

Preposterous? Not at all—not for the man and woman who are soul mates. Soul mates care about what is happening with each other. They set aside time to be emotionally available, listening to what the other person has to say. Soul mates treasure each other and refuse to take one another for granted. They know they are invaluable to each other and are keenly interested in one another's joys and sorrows. Nothing is mundane or mediocre.

*Create a bond of "into me see" (intimacy).* Soul-mate couples realize that emotions are the currency of intimate exchange. Emotional sharing is the bridge that brings couples together. When spouses share on a deep and personal level, a special connection occurs. We feel our mates' disappointments, their sadness, their concerns, and their excitements. When we empathize with our mates, they feel our care and an incredible resonance occurs.

Daphne Rose Kingma agrees that an emotional connection is of paramount importance.

> *Too many of us are emotional chickens, afraid to communicate what we are really feeling. Emotional chickens are afraid that what they disclose will be ignored, made fun of, or ridiculed, so rather than taking the risk of spitting it out—whatever it is—they just*

*keep quiet. . . . Being emotionally brave means that now, in spite of
the possible adverse effects, you will risk saying the things that may
leave you feeling exposed, and trust in a happy outcome.*[3]

*See your mate as a child of God.* When we see our mates as children of
God, with all of their good and their bad, we stop trying to control
them. We stop trying to make them who we'd like them to be. We
accept that they are separate from us and in a sense are only on loan
to us for a short time.

Soul mates allow each other room to grow, falter, make mistakes,
and be human. Soul mates realize they will disappoint each other at
times. But recognizing that this disappointment is part of the nature
of relationships, they accept these limitations.

## Wonder-Full

Wearing rose-colored glasses allows you to see your surroundings with
a sense of wonder. Optimists and opportunists always see the wonder
in life. They see opportunities in the midst of disappointment and
embrace every aspect of life.

I have a new grandson. His name is Caleb Joshua Hawkins, and
he is fabulous. Only a few weeks old, he is already beginning to take
in the world. His eyes dart around, looking left to right, right to left.
Don't tell him the world isn't wonderful, because it is.

Caleb is entering into a larger world filled with strife, and into a
smaller world filled with love and affection. I held him when he was
only a few hours old and immediately fell in love with him. I looked
into his dark eyes, and said clearly and calmly, "I love you." Tears formed
in my eyes as I gazed at this tiny and wonderful creation of God.

"How is it possible to love someone you don't know?" I said to
Christie. "How can you love someone who has given nothing back
to you? It is surreal."

"He is tiny and innocent, and will accept every bit of love you give
him," she said, smiling. "And we'll give him a lot of love."

Christie and I held hands as we left the hospital, and I left with
a feeling of love as immense as what I felt on the days my sons were
born—and that is a lot of love. I kept twisting in my mind the fact that

I loved this child who was virtually incapable of offering anything back to me. He was full of wonder, and I was too. How was this possible?

I think there is an inherent lesson in this experience with my new grandson that applies to rose-colored glasses and loving your mate so much that you become soul mates. I think there is a lesson in all of this about giving regardless of what you get back, knowing in your heart

**MUTUAL REACTION—MUTUAL ATTRACTION**
The way you react—either aggressively or lovingly—
is likely to lead your spouse to respond in the same manner.

that much will return to you. It seems to me that when we love much, our hearts become larger so that we're able to love even more. We were created with an ability to love, and our mates, even though they have flaws and limitations, are still immensely worthy of that love. Spouses love one another simply because they are who they are, and because they will accept one another's love. That's a pretty special thing.

As you think about your mate, imagine he or she is a child, full of wonder, desperately needing to be loved. Even with his or her limitations, your spouse has the same need for love and affirmation as you. Even if he or she is distant and struggling, your spouse still wants to be loved. Even if he or she is angry or exhibits unloving behavior, you can still see the potential in him or her. Don't cling to your current perceptions; entertain new possibilities. Think of your spouse as a repository for love, knowing that if you love him or her, both of you will grow larger. If you will look on your mate gently, with rose-colored glasses—perhaps not as he or she truly is but as he or she is capable of being—you will have done something of wonder.

## Embracing Possibilities

There's a pony in every pile of horse manure and endless possibilities in every marriage. You must simply believe and then move forward on that belief.

I haven't always been a believer. It's taken some tough times, some marital struggles, and some dark-colored days to come to the belief that there are possibilities and opportunities everywhere—yes, everywhere.

Rosamund Stone Zander and her husband, Benjamin Zander, conductor of the Boston Philharmonic Orchestra, have been instrumental in helping me believe. They tell an amusing story in their book, *The Art of Possibility*.

> *A shoe factory sends two marketing scouts to a region of Africa to study the prospects for expanding business. One sends back a telegram saying, "SITUATION HOPELESS STOP NO ONE WEARS SHOES." The other writes back triumphantly, "GLORIOUS BUSINESS OPPORTUNITY STOP THEY HAVE NO SHOES."*
>
> *To the marketing expert who sees no shoes, all the evidence points to hopelessness. To his colleague, the same conditions point to abundance and possibility.*[4]

This is a funny story, and one that we can readily relate to. How quick are we to see possibilities in situations, or more often, how quickly do we rule out the possibilities?

I see something similar quite often in my practice as a psychologist. Frequently I see opportunity where others see hopelessness.

A couple comes to me and shares their history of fighting and bickering. The casual observer, watching this couple engage in their arguing anywhere and everywhere, is quick to feel critical and utter the words, "Why do they put up with each other? They ought to split up." I observe this same couple and see possibilities. If they are able to practice the same negative behaviors again and again, there is nothing to prevent them from practicing positive behaviors again and again, with much more pleasurable results.

The Twelve Step program of Alcoholics Anonymous asks only three things of anyone wishing to join their group: to be honest, open, and willing. I ask the same of anyone coming to me for counseling. I know if a couple will come to me with their problems, as chronic and entrenched as they may be, if they are honest, open, and willing, they will see new possibilities.

I'm reminded of Nicodemus, who as part of the Jewish council was one of the few religious leaders of his day to be interested in Jesus. However, enjoying a prestigious position, he wasn't ready to risk it all to let his interests be known. So he came to Jesus in the night.

> *"Rabbi," he said, "we all know that God has sent you to teach us. Your miraculous signs are evidence that God is with you."*
> *Jesus replied, "I tell you the truth, unless you are born again, you cannot see the Kingdom of God."*
> *"What do you mean?" exclaimed Nicodemus. "How can an old man go back into his mother's womb and be born again?"*
> *Jesus replied, "I assure you, no one can enter the Kingdom of God without being born of water and the Spirit."*
> (John 3:2-5, NLT)

Nicodemus continued to doubt and question Jesus; however, it appears that his heart gradually changed, and he began to embrace Jesus' teachings. Though frightened of public ridicule, over time Nicodemus overcame his fear and followed Jesus.

The same Spirit that changed Nicodemus's heart is able to change your heart and mine. The same Spirit is able to awaken new possibilities not only in how we view our mates, but in how we treat them. One changed heart, one small behavior change, and soon we've begun a radical shift in perspective. This is the same transformation that takes place in moving from mate to soul mate.

## Weekly Quiz

We have the ability to choose to focus on what is wrong in the relationship or on what is right. We can decide every relationship struggle is an opportunity for positive change. What color glasses would you wear in the following situation?

Your mate gripes about the weekend filling up with obligations. You:

    a)  become defensive and forcefully tell him or her to stop complaining, since he or she agreed to the plans.

b) suggest sitting down and looking at your plans, exploring ways to see how you can loosen the schedule and find time for yourselves.

......................................................................................

## PUTTING IT INTO PRACTICE THIS WEEK

1. If you haven't already done so, take a few minutes to complete the exercise on page 22. Zero in on a difficulty in the past that you've moved beyond. How did you get past the irritation and anger? What positives came out of that experience?

2. If you currently feel as if you and your mate are at an impasse over an issue, take some time to look at it in a new way. What opportunity for growth does it offer? How could you turn a potential fight into a challenging opportunity for growth?

3. What could you and your spouse do to restore the wonder in your relationship this week? It doesn't need to be elaborate; anything that gets you thinking like a kid again—jumping in rain puddles, looking at the stars, popping popcorn and then sitting down together to watch a lighthearted movie—can remind you how much pleasure you can get together out of life.

4. When you catch yourself criticizing something your spouse says or does, ask yourself if there's another way to look at the situation.

# BRINGING OUT THE BEST QUALITIES OF YOUR SPOUSE

*Her smiles, her frowns, her ups, her downs, are second nature
to me now, like breathing out and breathing in.*
—Henry Higgins, commenting about Eliza Doolittle in *My Fair Lady*

## SIGNS THAT YOU NEED TO BRING OUT YOUR MATE'S BEST QUALITIES

1. You rarely thank your spouse when he or she completes a household task—after all, isn't that just his or her responsibility?
2. You believe in the principle of there being too much of a good thing—including time with your spouse, which is why you spend four nights out of seven apart.
3. The last time you tried to ask your spouse for something, one of you ended up sleeping on the couch.
4. You figure your spouse will always be there, so other people and things need to take priority right now.
5. You put more thought into deciding what to wear each day than in how you could meet your spouse's needs.

An improbable combination, Henry Higgins is the fastidious, exacting professor of phonetics and Eliza Doolittle, a street vendor selling flowers who has a strong Cockney accent.

Noticing Doolittle on the streets of London, Higgins, an irascible and impatient man, boasts to his friend, Colonel Pickering, that he can teach her impeccable English and pass her off as a duchess. The bet is on.

This is the theme of the hugely popular musical *My Fair Lady*, based on the book *Pygmalion* by George Bernard Shaw.

Through excruciatingly hard work at mastering proper English,

Eliza not only wins our hearts but the heart of Higgins as well. Though Eliza is the student, Henry learns a thing or two from her about how to treat people. His harsh work ethic is gradually transformed into a softer teaching style. Months of work finally pay off when she convincingly poses as an elegant duchess at an embassy ball.

The subplot is Higgins's growing attraction to Eliza. In one of the final scenes, Higgins, who has driven Eliza off with his abrupt, critical attitude, wistfully announces, "I've grown accustomed to her face."

The musical did more than win a handful of Tony Awards. It spawned the notion of the Pygmalion effect, more commonly known as the teacher-expectancy effect: students perform better when they are expected to do so. The Pygmalion effect leads students to internalize the expectations of their teachers. Students whose teachers have negative expectations of them internalize those negative presumptions, while students whose teachers have positive expectations internalize positive outlooks. This is not surprising, since when teachers are told certain students are bright and can perform at high levels, they treat those students differently. Intuitively we know that the labels we put on others or that are placed on us are cumbersome, limiting, and often wrong.

Taking the Pygmalion effect one step further, we see that it is possible, by altering our expectations of our spouses, to treat them in a

**THE PYGMALION EFFECT**
If you have positive expectations of your spouse, he or she is likely to internalize that and live up to your expectations.

way that brings out their best qualities. Just as Henry Higgins made a duchess out of Eliza Doolittle, we can make princes and princesses out of our mates. In fact, that is our strategy this week—we will begin to call forth the best qualities of our mates.

So far we've examined the pitfalls of wearing dark-colored glasses, which can leave us entrenched in disappointment, disillusionment, and resentment. We've also discovered that we may replace those dark-colored glasses with rose-colored ones, choosing to see the best in our mates. With this change of expectations, we "see" in our mates people of infinite worth, with possibilities of greatness and magnificence.

Now in our third week of transformational work, we take things one step further: we actually *call forth* the positive qualities we want to see in our mates, day in and day out. By sheer force of imagination and encouragement, we can bring out the best in our mate. Remarkable! We're not simply the recipient of our mates' moods or their generosity of spirit; we play an integral role in how they respond to us.

Before you can bring out your mate's best qualities, however, you must believe that it is within your power, and is even your responsibility, to do so. Instead of assuming a passive role in your relationship, you must embrace a whole new mind-set that recognizes that *you* have the ability to elicit the best qualities from your mate. *You* have the choice, either to anticipate and "see" your spouse's worst qualities or to imagine his or her best qualities and create a safe place for those qualities to be expressed.

## The Power of Imagination

I'll never forget my seventh grade algebra teacher, Mrs. McCormick from Mt. Baker Junior High School in Deming, Washington. A thin woman who appeared to be a hundred and three, Mrs. McCormick surprised our class with her warmth and gentleness. I had expected something far more critical from this slight, stooped woman who dressed in "old lady" clothes.

I didn't like math and had an attitude before even entering her room. Seeing this older woman, with more wrinkles than a Shar-Pei, I already believed she couldn't possibly teach me anything.

What I didn't take into consideration, however, was the power of Mrs. McCormick's imagination. She could see beyond my attitude, through my fear and intimidation, and well past my detachment. In short, she trusted in her ability to teach. My, how she could teach!

To my absolute surprise, Mrs. McCormick patiently introduced algebra to her awkward group of young teens. Amidst our snickers and disrespect, she stood firm that we were going to master algebra. Slowly, methodically, and enthusiastically, she shared mathematical principles. She smiled, teased, and taught—and I caught on to the subject. We all caught on. I surprised myself when I discovered I not only understood algebra, but I enjoyed it.

How did Mrs. McCormick do it? She did it *not* by embracing what she saw—a group of anxious, socially awkward kids very unexcited about algebra—but by imagining a group of kids who could get excited about learning. She looked at me and imagined a kid who could not only learn but who could become excited about what she was teaching. She was right.

Mrs. McCormick believed in and trusted her own abilities. She assumed she could call forth any innate aptitude her students had for math. *If David Hawkins can learn,* she must have thought, *then I can teach him.*

What if we took the same attitude about love with our mates?

*If Christie Hawkins can love,* I might imagine, *then I can help her love me. If she has the ability to be loving and kind and generous and encouraging, then with imagination and intentionality, I can call forth those traits toward me.* Christie *does* have the ability to be loving, kind, generous, and encouraging, and I do routinely call those traits out. It's greatly rewarding, by the way!

## Teaching Others How to Treat Us

Is it really true that I can teach people how to treat me well? Is it possible that I can imagine and instruct others on the fine art of being loving, kind, generous, and encouraging *to me*? Of course it is.

Again, this process first begins with the imagination. We have to know what it is we want to call forth from our mate. We must be able to specifically articulate those precise traits we see and value most. Let me offer an example of how one couple does this.

Jay and Michelle are friends of ours. Both are optimists by nature and have an intoxicating thirst for life. They have been married thirty years and have two grown children. Spending time with Jay and Michelle is a treat for Christie and me as we watch them act like newlyweds. In fact, they are so demonstrative with their affection that I've taken to watching them even more closely. One day not long ago I took Jay aside and posed a few questions I'd been dying to ask.

"You guys are so kind and tender to each other," I said. "What's the deal?"

"What do you mean?" he asked, appearing surprised.

"You and Michelle are so kind and tender to each other," I said again, a bit puzzled that he was surprised. "It's not normal, you know," I said, smiling.

"We came through a time in our marriage where things were stale," he said. "Nothing bad, mind you. But bland. We both felt ignored and unheard, and we vowed we were going to change. Maybe we're a bit different from others, but we believe we can make our marriage anything we want it to be. We want it to be good, so we make it good."

Just as I was going to comment, he continued.

"We knew we could continue on with the way things were because we're committed to each other. But we wanted to be more than just another couple who have been able to sustain a marriage. What's a marriage if it doesn't have heart and soul?" he asked.

"You're so right about that," I said. "But you make it sound so easy. If it were that easy, there'd be no divorces."

"There is one more thing that seems to make a difference," he said. "We asked each other how we wanted to be treated. We were very specific. Each of us had a list of qualities that were important to us, and we each felt that we could and would give our mate those things. We were clear that the qualities the other person needed were things we could and would give. We've stuck with that intentionality."

"Give me an example."

"Sure," he said. "I told Michelle that quality time alone with her was critical to me. I was tired of climbing the ladder of success but not having time with the one I love. I was very vulnerable and transparent with her. She's been great about giving that to me. She even suggested we reserve every Friday night as a date night. I was really pleased when she added that she would accompany me on business trips whenever possible."

"And what about her?" I asked.

"She said she wanted me to create more special times together. I'm doing that. I know how much she enjoys visiting art galleries, and I arrange a special outing every week or two. In fact, I notice that when

I give to her, she gives back to me naturally. It really doesn't take that much effort. One positive response seems to ignite a positive response in the other."

"What do you do when she gets too busy for you?" I asked.

"I sit down with her, look her in the eyes, and tell her I miss her. I tell her that I know she loves me and can give me more of herself and her time. I tell her that I'd like more of her. It always works."

"The way you just said that was very nice," I said. "You weren't critical of her, you weren't demanding, and you didn't judge her. You simply told her that you'd like more from her. You know, you guys are an inspiration to Christie and me."

## Letting Go of Limitations

Jay and I continued to talk about relationships. I realized that it wasn't simply his relationship with Michelle that impressed me. Jay is also a can-do kind of guy. Rather than seeing limitations, he sees possibilities.

He went on to explain that what he wanted from Michelle was something she was fully capable of giving. "It's not like I'm asking her to do something way beyond her abilities," he told me. "She can give me time and enjoys making it happen, so why not ask for it?"

This all seemed too simple. I have spent hours pondering that conversation. It all had to be more complex, I thought. If it is as simple as asking for what you need, confident that your mate has your best interests in mind, why aren't more couples blissfully happy?

One of the reasons, I surmised, has to do with limitations. Not that our mates are limited, but we limit what we ask for. We limit what we *believe* our mates are willing to give to us. We limit what we're willing to risk seeking from our mates. Frankly, we live in a self-created world of limitations.

One of the things that first attracted Janet to Ted was his obvious delight in his nieces and nephews. He regularly took them on outings, and at family gatherings he was always the first to join them in a game of football. Twelve years later, the couple has a young daughter of their own. Ted is now a busy accountant who comes home tired and regularly puts off his little girl's requests to play with her.

He doesn't appear to notice his daughter's dejected looks—but Janet does. However, she just bites her tongue, afraid that if she expresses her desire that Ted make more time for their child, he'll get angry and accuse Janet of not appreciating how hard he has been working to provide for them.

What do you think would happen if Janet believed that Ted was a good man who would respond to her gentle requests to spend more time one-on-one with their daughter? What would happen if you believed your mate was capable of being a loving, kind, generous, sensual, spiritual, exciting creature of God? What if you believed he or she wanted to give to you and is simply waiting to be asked to enter into a mutually giving relationship? Kind of mind-boggling, don't you think? Perhaps a key to abundant living is simply the art of invitation.

There is a hitch—if you're going to ask for the sun and moon from your mate, you have to be ready and willing to give it in return. That slowed you down a bit, didn't it? Relationships function best when they are mutually satisfying. When Janet meets Ted's deepest desire for respect and appreciation, he is ready and willing to respond to her request of him. When she is ready to be his soul mate, he is standing at the ready to be hers as well.

*But whenever I try to talk with my spouse about what I need, we get into an argument,* you might think. Don't be too quick to assume

---

**TIMING IS EVERYTHING**

Ask for what you need from your spouse at the right time and in the right way, being willing to give your spouse what he or she needs in return.

---

you'll never get what you want from your spouse. Could it be that you make your request in the wrong way, with the wrong tone, at the wrong time? If Janet confronts Ted at the front door as he comes home from work, accusing him of neglecting their child, Ted is likely to get angry and defend himself. However, if the next time she catches Ted coloring with their little girl, she smiles and tells him how happy it makes her to see them playing together, he is much more likely to heed her suggestion that he regularly make time to do things with their daughter.

Don't allow self-imposed limits to keep either you or your spouse from the best you have to give. Julia Cameron, author of *The Artist's Way*, believes we live with far too many limitations.

> One of the chief barriers to accepting God's generosity is our limited notion of what we are in fact able to accomplish. . . . We don't take ourselves—or God—seriously enough and so we define as grandiose many schemes that, with God's help, may fall well within our grasp. Remembering that God is my source, we are in the spiritual position of having an unlimited bank account.[1]

Cameron suggests we must stop being stingy with each other. Just as surely as we can stretch and believe in God's largesse, we can imagine the same from our mates. We can offer them gifts from our not-so-limited-as-we-might-think wells. We can also ask to receive from them.

## Recalling Your Mate's Best

In order to receive the best from your mate—which is what it takes to be a soul mate—you must first know what that is. You must be able to see it, feel it, imagine it, and then call it forth. Just as Mrs. McCormick was able to quickly look at her students and appreciate their capabilities, you must do the same with your mate.

One of the surest ways you can do this is by experience. Take a moment to answer these questions:

- What did you most admire in your mate when you met him or her? Be specific. Consider specifically those traits that made you want to be with this person again and again.
- What made your mate stand out from others you may have dated? What traits made him or her unique?
- What traits do you miss most when you are away from him or her for any period of time?

- How would you describe the perfect evening spent with your mate? What would you be doing? Reflect upon exactly what that evening would look like.

Let me answer those questions in regard to my wife. When I first met Christie, I admired her quick wit. In fact, since we had corresponded prior to actually meeting, I knew she was bright and funny. She didn't take herself too seriously, and I knew I would be comfortable with her.

After meeting her I wrote the following in my journal: "I've met a wonderful woman. She is cute, funny, and very easy to be with. We enjoyed each other's company and she seems to have many of the same values I have. I'm attracted to her and want to see her again."

Christie stood out from others I had dated by her attractive appearance and dedication to fitness, her solid faith and dedication to family, her easy laugh and willingness to spend quiet evenings together instead of always needing to be on the go.

When I'm away from her I miss her greeting me at the door, telling me she missed me and asking about my day. I miss snuggling with her on the couch as we share news of our days. I miss her huge smile.

My perfect evening with Christie begins with a moonlit walk on the beach. Next we enjoy a simple candlelight dinner in our cottage, followed by cuddling up as we read a book out loud together.

How does knowing this information help me call out the best in my mate? By identifying what drew me to her, I recognize what she can do now to continue to draw me to her. Also, through past experience I know Christie is still fully capable of offering these same blessings to me, and it is the combination of these blessings that makes her my soul mate. I know she desires to give to me and has my best interests in mind. I know she remains the same generous person I fell in love with, and given the right circumstances—primarily when I provide safety for her—she wants to freely give those gifts to me again and again.

While quite a bit of time may have passed since you and your spouse first met, believe that each of those traits that attracted you to one another are still there waiting to be called forth. Believe that together you and your mate can remember the best about each other and pave a path from mate to soul mate.

## How to Get the Best from Your Spouse

*Encourage generously*

One quality, more than any other, provides the right environment for your mate to display his or her best attributes. That quality is encouragement. No mate ever became a soul mate without being encouraged to become one.

Encouragement seems to be a lost art in today's world. How often do we forget to say thanks when our spouses do something kind for

---

**NEVER UNDERESTIMATE THE POWER OF ENCOURAGEMENT**
Behavior that is reinforced is replicated most often.

---

us? How many times do they perform a task, going out of their way for us, without our acknowledgement? Far too often.

Christie takes my shirts to the cleaners to have them laundered and starched. I try to let her know how much I appreciate clean, freshly laundered shirts. She lets me know that my appreciation makes the task more enjoyable. She tells me how much she appreciates me mowing our lawn. Knowing she values my efforts encourages me to complete the task.

We know that behavior is most often replicated if it is reinforced. If there is something your mate does that you appreciate, let him or her know. If there is something special your mate does that you would like to see continue, tell him or her. Smile, reach out, touch, and offer words of encouragement.

One of my favorite Scriptures is Ephesians 4:29: "Let everything you say be good and helpful, so that your words will be an encouragement to those who hear them." (NLT)

Think about it. What if we spoke only words of encouragement, and those words were tailored specifically to the individual needs of our mates? Can you imagine the power of our speech?

It's not so easy though, is it? If you are anything like me, every day feels like a race. From the moment my feet hit the floor, I feel like I'm running a marathon. I grab a quick breakfast, dash out the door, start seeing clients as soon as I get to my office, and manage the daily challenges of my private practice. By the time I drag my weary body home, I'm not the best version of myself. I soak up the encouragement of my wife like a sponge.

I need her to look at me and say, "You're my hero. Thank you for working so hard for us." I need her to look me in the eyes and tell me, "You're my man!" I still become giddy when she grabs me, gives me a huge hug, and tells me, "I got the best end of this deal." At those moments I would give her the moon on a silver platter if I could!

But as much as I love that kind of affirmation, I must not forget that Christie needs the same encouragement. Her needs may be a bit different, her areas of discouragement different from mine, yet the issue is the same—she needs encouragement for being who she is.

The key, as the apostle Paul says, is to recognize "what words will be an encouragment to those who hear them." We must know our mates' needs. We must be so tuned in to them that we know, beyond a doubt, where their hearts beat.

Encouragement, perhaps more than any other quality, brings out the best your spouse has to give. As an encouraging husband or wife, you compliment, support, and name specific actions and qualities that you appreciate. When you mutually give the best to one another, you're no longer simply mates; you're soul mates.

## Create safety

Safety is often underrated and misunderstood in relationships. But in my experience, safety is absolutely critical to bringing out your mate's best qualities. Without the security of knowing that what he or she shares will be appreciated and respected—no one will share from his or her most vulnerable self.

God created us with a natural desire to be intimate and to share deeply with each other. However, this intimacy cannot occur without complete safety. We must be assured that we will be loved, valued, and accepted no matter what. We must know that we can be vulnerable and that vulnerability requires significant risk. In order for any of us to take that risk, we must believe we are completely safe.

What exactly do I mean by safety? Here are a few of the qualities that comprise safety in a relationship:

*Caring about what is important to your mate.* In order for your mate to care about what is important to you, you must care about what is important to him or her. If you enter the relationship with a "give to

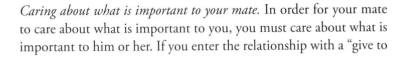

**SAFETY FIRST**
You won't get the best from your spouse until he or she knows your love, respect, and acceptance are unconditional.

me" attitude, without expecting to give equally in return, your mate will either withhold from you or burn out from giving and not receiving. Your spouse must know, beyond a shadow of a doubt, that you are interested in what is important to him or her.

Christie enjoys spending time with her adult children and really appreciates my efforts to make her children feel welcomed in our home. I let her know verbally, and with actions, that I recognize and appreciate her close and affectionate relationship to her children. Can you think of ways you might convey an understanding and caring attitude for what is important to your mate?

*Showing that your spouse's feelings are safe with you.* Feelings, perhaps the most vulnerable aspect of our being, must have a safe resting place. Your mate must know that his or her feelings will not be judged, ridiculed, or shamed but will be protected and embraced by you.

*Knowing that he or she will receive time from you.* Your mate must know he or she will not be hurried, stifled, or ignored. Spouses must know that both partners will give one another the time and space to be who they are. In the safety of *kairos* time, which is unscheduled time to simply be, you both will feel safer to share yourselves with each other.

*Encouraging openness.* In order for your mate to give of him- or herself freely, he or she must sense and know you care about him or her. Your spouse must be encouraged to be open, asked to share more, and be positively reinforced for the risks he or she takes to be open and vulnerable.

*Sensing you are a kindred soul.* We share most freely with those we feel we've known a lifetime. Regardless of whether we have known someone for decades or for just fifteen minutes, intuition tells us whether that person can be trusted.

Several weeks ago I spent a short time with Cec Murphey, a celebrated author and wise man. I discussed some of my deepest secrets with him, even though I hardly know him. I'm not sure why I was willing to confide in him; I just knew I could. Perhaps it was the way he gave me his undivided attention when I was talking. Maybe it was his enthusiasm as we discussed our respective writing projects. It could have been his unpretentious spirit. Though I cannot say for sure what about him freed me to open up, what I do know is that he provided a sense of safety for me.

How well do I provide that kind of safety for my wife? Since I want to bring out her best qualities, I must provide a safe place for her to foster those qualities. I must set the stage for her to bring her most treasured gifts—the gifts that comprise her being. For example, because I value her kindness and quick wit, after a get-together with friends at our home, I can compliment her on her ability to make our guests relax and feel at home.

What that means for you is this: You can call forth the best qualities of your mate, and you must do this if you are to be soul mates. You must provide an atmosphere in which your spouse feels safe and encouraged to be him- or herself.

## Anticipate with hope

Anticipation—the expectation that something good will result from our words and actions—is not just the title of a song Carly Simon made famous in the 1970s; anticipation is another key element in calling for the best from your mate.

I remember the months prior to the birth of our grandson, Caleb.

As grandparents, we were waiting on the sidelines, doing anything we could to create a welcoming atmosphere for this newest member of the Hawkins family.

I became a doting father to my grown son. "Have you decorated the baby's room yet? Have you purchased the crib and baby clothes? Have you arranged to be off work for a few weeks?"

I think he and Jacqueline, his wife, began to tire of my questions. "We're ready, Dad," he finally said impatiently. They had made plans, and now they, too, were simply waiting for this ultimate gift. Anticipation.

I'm also reminded of the words of Joshua as he was instructed to lead the children of Israel across the Jordan River into the Promised Land. Remember that the Israelites had been waiting years to enter this land. The day before entering it, Joshua paused in anticipation of the incredible event, offering the following instruction: "Purify yourselves, for tomorrow the LORD will do great wonders among you" (Joshua 3:5, NLT).

Joshua reminded the people that something momentous was about to happen, and they must be prepared. This wasn't just another leg in their journey—this was it! They needed to be ready for something amazing, something spectacular. They needed to set themselves apart from their everyday life and everything unclean before they embarked on this journey of a lifetime. They needed to engage in certain rituals that would prepare their hearts and minds to receive everything God had ready for them.

How often we skip over this short verse when reading this great story. But it is an important verse about anticipation, consecration, and preparation. It raises certain questions: Are you ready to receive the gifts prepared for you? Just as the Israelites had to be prepared for all God had promised them, have you prepared yourself for all that your mate is ready to give you? Have you done your part to call forth the best in your mate? It's one thing to want the best your mate has to offer, and quite another to be fully prepared to receive and offer your best to your mate.

I've noticed that I must be a positive recipient of Christie's gifts. I must not only watch for her tenderness toward me but I must also receive it with warmth and appreciation. I must ensure that when she gives me gifts of kindness, affection, and love, she knows the value of her gifts. This requires preparation on my part so that when the moment of giving arrives, I'm ready and emotionally available to receive it.

Consecration is a biblical concept involving preparation for something incredible from God. Consecration is about making space in your life for new growth. We understand we're on a journey, like the children of Israel, ready for something new in our lives. We're set apart, consecrated to a new relationship, a new purpose, and perhaps even a new identity. Far from being a passive process, consecration is very active. We don't just sit back anticipating these new gifts coming from our mates—we change our hearts, minds, and perhaps even our identities.

### Express gratitude

While encouragement, safety, and anticipation are necessary to bring out your mate's best qualities, gratitude keeps them coming.

"Thanks," Christie said, reaching over to give me a peck on my forehead. "I appreciate you helping with the dishes."

"Of course," I replied, barely looking up from my desk where I was writing.

"I really mean it," she continued.

"You're certainly welcome," I said, taking a moment to look up and smile at her.

This has become part of our routine. We try never to take one another for granted, which seems so common in marriages. Rather than simply expecting the other person to meet our needs or be gracious to us, we each go out of our way to express appreciation. Soul mates make the most of these small, incidental opportunities to reinforce the very qualities that make them so close.

Alexandra Stoddard writes eloquently about appreciation and gratitude. "Life is a joy when we stop racing around in a feverish search for a new, vague 'something' out there. When we live in a state of endless expectation of what could be, we never experience exaltation in what is: being alive to what is here for us every day."[2]

We must apply this same concept of gratitude to our mates. We must find the balance between calling forth the best in our mates

while also seeing the best that is already taking place. We must anticipate and prepare for something better, something more, while also
exalting in what is here now.

Is it possible you have begun to take for granted some of the fine
qualities you appreciate in your mate? How, exactly, are those qualities demonstrated? Don't just notice them; comment on them and
show your profound appreciation of them.

During a recent trip to South Carolina I was given a lesson in
graciousness and gratitude from a most unlikely source. I had flown
into Greenville and then checked into my hotel, where I prepared
for a television broadcast the next day. After breakfast the following
morning I went to the lobby to wait for the driver who would take
me to the studio. At precisely the prearranged time, a teenager wearing baggy pants and an earring strolled through the lobby. I glanced
at him and looked back down at my morning paper, assuming he
couldn't be my driver.

"Sir," the teenager said, "are you Dr. Hawkins?"

"Yes," I said, wondering what he wanted.

"I'm your driver, sir, and am ready to take you to the studio. My
name is Neil. We're so pleased you came all this way to be with us.
May I help you with your luggage?"

Still trying to decide what I thought of this young man, I told him
I could carry my overnight bag.

"No, sir, please allow me to carry your luggage. It's our pleasure
to have you come to be with us. My grandmother is so excited you're
here. My car is waiting right outside."

Still trying to figure this kid out, I allowed him to take my
luggage.

"I hope you had a pleasant night. Did you sleep well?" he said as
we walked to his car.

I couldn't help but smile at Neil's graciousness. All my stereotypes
were flying out the window. Where had this kid learned to talk like
this? Was he being genuine, or had he rehearsed this for his grandmother, the host of the program I would be on?

We walked outside where his Mustang, which he proudly showed
off, was rumbling. He carefully placed my luggage in the backseat of
his car, revved his engine, and headed for the studio.

Neil continued his graciousness all the way to the studio, asking about Washington, my books, and my life. Not once did he turn the conversation onto himself.

So much for my narrow belief about young people with earrings, baggy pants, and loud cars! Here was a young man well versed in the art of showing appreciation. I felt honored, respected, and invited.

This was an unexpected moment when I felt overwhelmed by grace. When I first saw Neil, I assumed he was a kid with an attitude. I wasn't prepared for a kid with genteel manners and dignity. But his style exuded graciousness, and I couldn't help but respond in kind.

Be honest with yourself: Are you more likely to disregard your mate, taking a quick glance now and then and quickly concluding he or she no longer has anything to offer? Or are you constantly looking for and complimenting that smile, that attitude, that quality that drew you to your mate in the first place? This is one of the most powerful lessons soul mates teach us: we have opportunities every day to appreciate graciousness and to respond graciously. It is in this wonderful space that we call out the best in each other.

## Weekly Quiz

Are you beginning to recognize your ability to bring out the best qualities in your spouse? No longer passive and simply waiting for good gifts, you anticipate positive changes. You watch for opportunities to amplify and enjoy positive interactions.

Here's your chance to apply this week's principle of bringing out the best in your mate:

Your mate is in a particularly happy mood and becomes playful with you. His or her timing is not perfect, however, and you initially find his or her behavior "silly," partly because you're still thinking about complications at the office. You

   a) shrug off your spouse's playfulness, letting him or her know
      this is not the best time to have a bit of fun.

b) seize the opportunity, set aside your worries, and engage fully with your mate, enjoying the moment.

...........................................................................................

## PUTTING IT INTO PRACTICE THIS WEEK

1. This week, make it a point to "catch" your mate doing something you appreciate. Then let your spouse know how much his or her words or action meant to you.

2. What do you want most from your mate? After you've jotted down your thoughts, ask yourself, can I be more specific? Once you have both come up with one or two ways the other person could make you feel most valued and appreciated, discuss your lists.

3. How can you express gratitude to your spouse in a way that will be most meaningful for him or her? If you're not sure, think back to situations when your spouse clearly appreciated your response, or ask him or her directly.

# REMEMBERING THE REASONS YOUR MATE LOVES YOU

*A thousand words will not leave so deep an impression as one deed.*
—Henrik Ibsen

## SIGNS THAT YOU NEED TO REMEMBER WHY YOUR MATE LOVES YOU

1. You're more concerned about impressing your next door neighbors than impressing your mate.
2. You have no idea what drew your spouse to you in the first place—although you're pretty sure it *wasn't* your smooth opening line.
3. You just wish your mate would give you more room to breathe.
4. You don't feel any need to be on "good behavior" around your spouse. After all, you promised to love each other for better or for worse!
5. You feel timid or uncertain around your mate.

When I started dating again a number of years ago, it was not unusual for me to spend Saturday afternoon polishing my sports car, getting a haircut, and even pressing the clothes I'd be wearing that evening. Preparation for the date began hours before leaving my driveway. By the time I left home, I was ready.

Being a mindful dater, I wanted to make a positive impression. But it was more than that. I didn't want to present a slick image that would vanish twenty minutes after a woman met me. I wanted my date to see the best I had to offer. I knew full well that I could impress someone for a moment, but that it would take consistent energy and intentionality to impress someone over a period of time.

Not only was I mindful about my first impression, but I was mindful of the first impression my date made on me. I was making an effort and hoped she would do the same. I prided myself in being able to gauge a person's character, her strengths as well as her weaknesses, and I suspected anyone I might be interested in would be able to do the same with me. This turned out to be true.

I pulled up in front of Christie's house for our first night out on a crisp January evening. Though it was the dead of winter, when my sports car would normally have been garaged, I wanted to make the best impression possible. I had spent the day washing and waxing the car and then headed to her place to pick her up for a movie. I considered my assets in pursuing her:

I am a genuinely nice guy.
I have a warm and charming personality.
I am a Christian.
I am goal oriented.
I have many interests, including music, sailing, hiking, and reading.
I am fairly good looking.
I am sincere and honest.
I am a good conversationalist.

Aware of those traits, I made my way to Christie's front door. She greeted me warmly, and we had a wonderful evening. We enjoyed the movie and the time we spent talking afterward. I discovered fairly quickly that Christie is genuinely a nice person with a warm and charming personality. I could tell she was goal oriented and that we shared many similar interests and a Christian faith. Did I mention she is also cute, bright, sincere, honest, and a wonderful conversationalist?

You probably won't be surprised to hear that I thoroughly enjoyed our first, second, and third dates. In fact, we decided early on to date only one another to see if there was a chance for this relationship. And as you know by now, Christie and I are now happily married.

## We Quickly Forget

Christie and I got off to a great start. We matched on all the critical issues. I liked her, and she liked me. What could possibly go wrong?

Not much, truthfully, since we were dedicated to maintaining the traits that made us attractive to each other. However, I'd be lying if I didn't say there have been a few touchy moments—all because we momentarily forgot why we were attracted to each other.

Initially charming and an astute listener, I eventually felt too busy to listen to her, and we hit our first bump. Feeling a bit smug about Christie's feelings for me, I became complacent. I forgot some of the reasons why I was attracted to her, but more important, *I forgot why she was attracted to me*—and that is my next secret for bringing out the best in your mate. You must—absolutely must—remember why you won your mate's heart initially.

Consider what happens when we forget why our mates dropped everything to settle into our camp. Reflect for a few moments on what naturally occurs when we allow ourselves to forget why our mates fell in love with us.

*We stop nurturing those admirable traits.* When we forget the precise reasons our spouses fell in love with us, we stop practicing some qualities that are very important to our marriages. We become complacent, settling into other, less admirable traits. Instead of remaining sensitive and attentive, at times we allow our less attractive traits (our shadow sides) to dominate, which weakens our connection with our spouses.

*We stop nurturing the admirable traits in our mates.* Once we settle into mediocrity, our spouses sometimes settle into mediocrity as well.

........................................................................................

**USE IT OR LOSE IT**
If you don't consciously remember and practice
those traits that drew your spouse to you, you will
inevitably lapse into less admirable behavior.

........................................................................................

There is a natural tendency for both of us to settle, which drains much of the excitement from our marriage.

Recently Christie and I sat down and reevaluated our goals for the next few months. I knew Christie was tired from a recent move and needed some downtime. She knew I needed uninterrupted time to write to complete this book on time. Together we planned a weeklong getaway that would meet her need for relaxation and my need for quiet. It would have taken less effort just to stay home and try to keep out of one another's way, but we each wanted to give the other what was needed most—and find a way to draw closer during a busy season.

*We allow ourselves to settle into comfortable but unhealthy traits.* Having accepted mediocrity, we slowly become accustomed to this style of living. Like precious silver that tarnishes if it's not polished, our life together becomes dull and lifeless. The shine fades, along with the love we felt for each other.

Christie and I regularly talk about how special each of us is to the other. We want to take care not to settle and take each other for granted.

## A Growing Fuzziness

Recently I met with Stan and Cindy, who have been married twenty years. They make a handsome couple; both are impeccably dressed professionals. Cindy is an articulate sales representative, and Stan is a hardworking insurance agent, handling a large client load with his firm. Both are successful in the business arena yet faltering in the relationship realm.

I listened as each told me about their relationship. They admitted that busyness had sapped their energies even as it brought them enormous wealth. While they enjoyed many luxuries, they were feeling more and more depleted relationally. They wanted to bring the fire back into their marriage.

"What do you think made Cindy fall in love with you?" I asked Stan.

He stammered at first, seemingly perplexed by the question.

"Well, uh . . . I was ready for you to ask me why I fell in love with Cindy," he said, smiling. "Why she fell for me, well, that's a tough question."

"Why is that?" I asked.

"I guess because I don't give it much thought," he continued. He turned to Cindy.

"So why did you fall in love with me?" he asked.

"Nope," I said, "not so quick. I really want you to think about why she fell in love with you. What was it about you that made her forget about all others and choose you?"

Both Cindy and Stan were chuckling at this point, surprised at how easy it is to explain what they liked about each other and how

...........................................................................................

**DON'T SETTLE**
Once you and your spouse expect mediocrity from one another, you're likely to settle into comfortable but unhealthy traits that will suck the life from your marriage.

...........................................................................................

difficult it is to name the qualities that had led the other person to choose him or her. Since they didn't spend time contemplating these traits, naturally they spent little time cultivating them.

"So, Stan," I repeated, "what are those traits that Cindy first admired?"

He threw out a few ideas, some of which hit the mark and some of which missed widely.

"I guess I can't be too critical," Cindy said cautiously. "I'm sitting here wondering what it was about me that made Stan fall in love with me, and I'm going blank."

"It's easy to miss the mark," I offered reassuringly. "We don't spend much time thinking about or cultivating those traits within ourselves. Once we've captured our mate, we often give up the pursuit. We stop putting bait on the hook, so to speak, so it's no surprise we stop catching anything.

"I wonder what would happen, Stan, if you were to bring back those traits that made Cindy fall in love with you. Any guesses?"

Stan smiled, reaching for Cindy's hand.

"I bet she'd love it," he said. Cindy nodded in agreement.

## Maintaining the Pursuit

What would happen if I acted as if each day with my wife was our first date by listening attentively to her, opening the door for her, and looking my best? I wish I maintained that level of focus, that singularity of purpose. Too often I drift. I forget that I must win my mate's heart again and again, day in and day out.

In his book *Wild at Heart*, John Eldredge reminds men that we must be relentless and never give up the pursuit of the woman in our lives. We must captivate our bride's heart over and over again. Our mates deserve the best we can offer—repeatedly. We must "bait our hook," so to speak, to win them over.

My father-in-law is an avid fisherman. He rises early to prepare his boat and talks excitedly about lures, downriggers, and test line. Vern is not content simply to purchase fish bait at the store—he uses his own special concoction to lure his fish. He is focused and dedicated, knowing that he is matching wits with a wily creature.

With so much on the line, you might think we'd work as hard at "keeping our mates on the hook" as we do at our fishing and hunting pursuits. You might think we'd keep our dating skills sharp, always ready to impress our mates. But such isn't the case. We become careless and perhaps even reckless.

Author Thomas Moore helps us understand why we become careless. "As strong as the yearning for attachment is, there is obviously something else in us that yearns for solitude, freedom, and detachment. Our examination of relationships must include both sides of this spectrum and embrace the tension that may exist as we try to give attention to both."[1]

Hmmm.

Moore suggests that we have a push-pull relationship with our mates. As much as we want attachment, we also want independence. This, of course, is not a new insight. We all feel the tension between drawing close and pushing away from those close to us.

As I thought about Moore's observation, I wondered if it helped explain why I "forget" to nurture the very qualities that made Christie fall in love with me. Is it part of the reason for my carelessness when it comes to being the charming and loving man I know I can be? Maybe so. Just as I often feel the urge to connect with Christie, I must be aware that sometimes I feel the urge to push her away. Failing to understand those urges can lead to trouble.

Acknowledging our innate tendency toward independence is

important. While it is never an excuse for a lack of intimacy, it may play a role in our lack of effective pursuit of our mates and must be managed. It is important to keep an open dialogue between you and

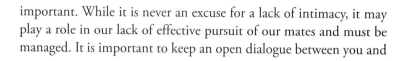

**TUG OF WAR**

As much as we want to be close to our spouses, we also crave our independence. Soul mates have learned to balance their need for personal space with their commitment to connection.

your mate. This will ensure your connection remains strong and alive. Don't be afraid to ask your mate how he or she feels about your connection to one another.

## Spaces in Our Togetherness

Appreciating the desire and need for space, we must manage the level of intimacy in our marriages carefully. Pushing away recklessly from our mates can lead to disaster. If we maintain our pursuit of our mates while also honoring our need to be alone, we will have thriving, robust marriages.

Kahlil Gibran, in his book *The Prophet*, first made me aware of this notion of "spaces in togetherness." I was floored when I first read his words: "But let there be spaces in your togetherness and let the winds of the heavens dance between you. Love one another but make not a bond of love: let it be rather a moving sea between the shores of your souls."[2]

Gibran's words offer something critically important—an explanation of why we need not pursue our mates at certain times. It is okay to suspend the hunt but not to sabotage it. It's fine to rest from the pursuit but not to abandon it. We must give ourselves permission to pursue independent goals and dreams and then come back together to share our experiences.

Christie and I are vigilant about creating time together as well as creating time apart. She knows I need times of solitude to fuel my writing, as well as time for writing itself. I also know she needs time to pursue her interests, such as reading, managing our home, and tending to her relationship with her children.

Time apart, of course, can make time together more incredible. The spaces in your togetherness can make being together even more magical. So there is a time to remember why your mate fell in love with you, and there is a time to rest from that remembering. In your resting, however, there is never a time for forgetting why he or she fell in love with you. Be careful with this balance.

## Careless and Reckless

Sadly, too many couples become careless in their treatment of one another. They have a casual attitude, taking each other for granted.

What does taking each other for granted mean? What happens when we become reckless in our pursuit of one another? In short, we act indiscriminately, kind and caring one minute, aloof and indifferent the next. We seek closeness and then recklessly create distance. Is it any wonder couples fail to bring out the best in each other in such an unsafe environment?

I was touched during a poignant moment in a recent marriage session with Stan and Cindy, whom I talked about earlier in this chapter. Cindy had been sharing about the distance she felt from Stan.

"I've been holding myself back from you," she said, looking into Stan's eyes. "Because you seem preoccupied, I don't often share my heart anymore. You used to care about everything I said, every hurt I experienced, every thought I had, but I don't sense that anymore."

For a moment, Stan seemed to tune in to Cindy. Just when I thought he might connect with her through a look or word, he suddenly, and almost dramatically, turned away and looked at me. I caught Cindy's eyes as she winced from his rejection. She began to cry.

"What did I do?" he asked, with sincere confusion.

"I need to feel safe with you," Cindy said, crying more profusely. "I need to know that when I'm vulnerable, like I was right then, you'll be there for me."

"I'm so sorry," Stan said, rubbing her shoulder. "I don't want to hurt you, and I sure want to provide that safe place for you to land. Please forgive me."

The three of us sat quietly for a time. "This is what I miss the most," Cindy finally said. "You were always so soft and tender with me, and I know you want to be that way again."

"I still am soft and tender, Cindy," Stan said gently. "That Stan is still alive and well and wants you to know you can be vulnerable with me. I want you to trust me with those kinds of feelings again."

Stan didn't mean to be reckless with Cindy's feelings. He wasn't intentionally disregarding them. When he turned away from her in my office, he wasn't being true to who he wanted to be and could be. In some ways Stan wasn't being Stan. He had become careless, insensitive in small ways. This incident in my office, however, reminded him that each moment of insensitivity, each instance of minute rejection, pushed Cindy away.

Relating is serious business. Bringing out the best in each other means maintaining a safe landing place for each other's feelings and consistently (not perfectly) being the best you can be.

I have come to know Stan well. He is a kind, gentle man with a quick wit and an engaging laugh. When I talk with him about ways to reignite his marriage, he looks at me intently. I know he wants his marriage to be everything it can be.

In many ways, when Stan remembers the reasons Cindy fell in love with him, he finds his way back to himself. When he recalls those magnanimous qualities that are integral to who he is, Stan will begin acting with *integrity*—a word that stems from the word *whole*. Rather than allowing himself to be distracted and separated from his true self, Stan needs to find himself again.

This task, however, doesn't belong only to Stan. Cindy must learn to act with integrity as well. She needs to be true to herself. Instead of silently pushing away from Stan when she feels rejected, she needs to have the courage to tell Stan she feels hurt. Instead of busying herself with other pursuits when she really wants to connect, she must be clear about her desires. She must have the strength to pursue what is most important to her.

Much of the work I'm doing with Stan and Cindy is designed to foster their integrity so they are acting whole and consistent with their personal values. They tell me they value each other. I ask them to behave in ways that are consistent with those values. They tell me they want to remember why their mate fell in love with them. I ask them to behave in the ways that first made their mate love them. I confront them when they behave in ways inconsistent with those qualities.

You might remember the apostle James's insights into integrity and the importance of being true to our values. He offers this counsel: "Do not waver, for a person with divided loyalty is as unsettled as a wave of the sea that is blown and tossed by the wind" (James 1:6, NLT).

Consider this truth: In order to have the deeply satisfying marriage you want, you must act in ways consistent with "your best self." In my own life, I always want to be the man who took the time to polish his car, open the car door, and listen attentively in a desire to win his mate. That is the true David. I can easily become distracted, careless, and reckless, but those faults aren't consistent with the real me. They certainly aren't consistent with the David who won Christie's heart years ago.

## Savoring

It's been said that much of winning at the game of life is simply showing up. This is true. So much of bringing out the best in your mate and cultivating a fabulous marriage occurs by showing up—completely, fully, and without distraction. Being present to your mate adds richness and vitality to your relationship.

We show up by remembering why our mate fell in love with us and embracing those qualities. Then we act on them. We keep our mates, and the reasons they care for us, front and center. But we can take things a step further. We can savor those qualities and allow them to develop even further.

The technique of savoring actually comes from the notion of delighting in a particular quality in a food or beverage, whether taste, texture, or even aroma. Recently Christie cooked me a particularly fine steak with asparagus. Savoring the meal, I commented on how juicy and tender the steak was. She had cooked it medium rare, just the way I like it, and I fully appreciated the taste of the meal, as well as her efforts on my behalf.

We can also savor an experience, remembering an event that was especially meaningful to us. We savor it by remembering various aspects of the occasion. Perhaps we remember the music that was playing, the people who were in the room, or the feeling it gave us. We play the scene over in our minds, enjoying different aspects of the event.

During a recent counseling session with Stan and Cindy, I applied the concept of savoring, giving Stan the following instructions: "I want you to list every single trait that made Cindy fall in love with

........................................................................................

**ACCENTUATE THE POSITIVE**

Remembering and savoring what your spouse loves about you requires you to intentionally continue wooing your spouse. It's more about you changing than your spouse.

........................................................................................

you. Then, looking at that list, I want you to amplify each trait, embellishing its highlights. I want you to embrace, amplify, and then demonstrate that trait."

I offered Stan an example from my own life: "I know that Christie fell in love with my chivalry," I said. "She loves when I open the door for her, wait for her before beginning to eat, and offer to help with tasks around our home. When I savor this quality, I imagine myself doing each of those things. I imagine myself being gallant and charming, waiting on her and making her feel like a princess. I imagine her smiling at me as I enjoy serving her. This is savoring the wonderful qualities we have inside."

Stan looked at me and then offered an example from his life. "Okay, so if I'm getting this, I'd relish the way I draw Cindy out when I sit and look at her as she's sharing her heart. I'd savor how I look into her eyes, letting her know I'm getting what she's telling me. I know she likes that. I'd reflect on how it feels to have her look back warmly at me. Do I have it?"

"You've got it," I told him. "I believe in you, Stan. I believe you want to be the best person you can be, and I know if you do that, Cindy will be madly in love with you all over again."

Cindy, who had heard this entire discussion, gave Stan a cheery "thumbs up" sign.

## Why Self-Confidence Matters

I still distinctly remember leaving my house to go to Christie's for the first time. I remember the care I took getting ready. I remember my feeling of excitement. I remember my positive attitude.

Can you sense the importance of the self-confidence I felt that night? Do you see that self-confidence, far from being a bad thing, is actually healthy? Self-confidence is that inner quality that allows me to appreciate what I have to offer and then to offer it. If I am acting with integrity, offering what I have to give, more often than not it will be accepted.

Self-confidence breeds success. It was in imagining success that I was able to present my best qualities to Christie. It was as I believed in myself that I was able to take risks, presenting myself to her completely and honestly. Being self-confident, I didn't hold myself back.

As you reflect on your skills and abilities, answer a few simple questions:

1. Do you know your strengths?
2. Do you embrace them and appreciate them?
3. Do you feel confident in displaying them to others?
4. Do you share them regularly with your mate?
5. If not, why not?

Now let's shift gears just a bit. Are you aware of any weak areas you need to strengthen? As you consider them, remember that behind every weakness is an opportunity for improvement.

1. What is your greatest relational weakness?
2. What impact does that weakness have upon your mate?
3. What are you currently doing to improve that area?

Finally, let's take the next step toward building a bridge to the benefit. Is your mate asking you to be a more active conversationalist? Take action to strengthen this weakness. Is he or she asking you to bring more creativity to your activities together? Consider some possibilities to spice up your life like you did in the early days of your relationship. Consider how you might take your weakness and turn it into a strength.

1. What is the hidden opportunity in your weakness?
2. What are some practical ways of turning your weakness into a strength?
3. Make a concrete plan now to do that.

Can you feel the importance of this issue? You are not doing yourself or your mate any favors by holding back on the best you can offer. Settling for weaknesses, instead of building them into strengths, does you no good. Being timid, insecure, or uncertain does no one any good. Both you and your mate need you to step forward and offer the best you can be.

## The Best Version of You

Only moments ago I offered Christie the I-want-to-chat-with-you-and-hear-how-your-day-is-going-today David. In a ten-minute phone conversation, Christie and I cheerfully reviewed how the day had gone so far. When I saw her picture come up on my cell phone, I was immediately excited and happy to hear from her. I chose to give her my best self. It was easy to do.

Remembering and savoring the reasons your mate loves you is about being the best version of you. It is about being the best you are fully capable of being, the best that God has made you to be.

Of course, we each have numerous renditions of ourselves. I am very aware that in addition to being charming and gallant, I can be testy and self-centered. In addition to being sensitive and caring, I can be distant and insensitive. For every redeeming feature I have, there are numerous aspects that are troublesome at best.

Being the best version of myself isn't always easy, especially if I've had a long day and feel irritable. When I'm tired and want to push away from Christie, it is tempting to be a bad version of myself. When I'm hungry and lonely and frustrated, I'm tempted to lapse into a bad version of myself. I always have a choice about the matter. When I'm at my weakest, I can remember that God loves me even more than Christie does and can give me the power to be the best version of myself.

What is critical to remember, however, is that I can choose which version of myself I want to be. I am the one who decides which David I will present to Christie when we greet each other at night. You also get to choose which version of yourself you will present to your mate.

This is powerful stuff. You have power to start a cascade of positive or negative feelings between the two of you. The choice is yours. You have the power to initiate a warm and engaging conversation or a stifled and hostile conversation. Again, the choice is yours. It really is that simple.

## Weekly Quiz

How are you doing at remembering and savoring why your mate fell in love with you? Are you able to name those qualities that made him or her find you irresistible?

How would you handle this situation?

Your mate lets you know he or she wants more zest in your marriage. He or she recalls all the fun, adventurous dates you planned for the two of you before your marriage. In addition, your spouse has been reading magazines and comparing your marriage unfavorably to the ones he or she reads about. You

a) become defensive and let him or her know that all marriages lose their spark over time. You insist dreams of a better marriage are unrealistic and let your spouse know he or she has got to lower his or her sights.

b) listen carefully to what he or she is saying, determined to understand exactly what qualities your spouse is missing in your marriage. You then set out to recreate them.

## PUTTING IT INTO PRACTICE THIS WEEK

1. What drew you and your mate to one another? If your spouse is willing, sit down together this week and see if you can recall the qualities that attracted you to one another.

2. Plan at least one way you will intentionally "pursue" your mate this week as you put into action those qualities that drew them to you in the first place. (For instance, since Cindy is drawn to her husband when he talks with her face-to-face, Stan might take her out to dinner with the express purpose of asking her about her week.)

3. Spouses will naturally feel an internal tug between their desire for intimacy and for independence. Do you see that dynamic at work within your own marriage? Explain.

4. This week observe how much time outside of work you and your spouse spend together. If you spend more time apart pursuing separate interests, talk about why that is. Consider scheduling a "standing date" with your spouse each week.

# GIVING UP DISTRACTIONS TO THE DREAM

*I press on toward the goal to win the prize for which God
has called me heavenward in Christ Jesus.*
—Philippians 3:14

## SIGNS THAT YOU NEED TO GIVE UP DISTRACTIONS TO THE DREAM

1. The last time you and your spouse shared a dream was when he or she showed up in your recurring nightmare of Godzilla chasing you through the streets of Manhattan.
2. You find yourself seeking pleasure and meaning outside your marriage.
3. When you think about your future together, you're not excited to see what lies next.
4. Sure, you want to improve your marriage—right after you win that big work promotion that will land you a corner office.
5. When your mate has a big success or is inspired by a new idea, you're not the first one he or she wants to tell. In fact, you fall somewhere between Great-aunt Peggy and the dog.

Before becoming an international hero, Sir Edmund Hillary, the first man to scale Mt. Everest, lived in obscurity as a beekeeper in Auckland, New Zealand.

Hillary noted in his account of the climb, *The Ascent of Everest*, that he never set out to climb the world's highest peak. It was only after a series of successful smaller climbs that he began to believe that he might be up to the challenge—a challenge that had never been successfully completed. In fact, numerous noted climbers had died attempting to scale Mt. Everest. Between 1920 and 1952, seven major expeditions failed to reach the summit.

One thing becomes clear as you read about Hillary's famous climb: it took incredible mental acuity to accomplish this feat. He could not be distracted; he dared not be distracted, as there were any number of problems that could prove fatal. If he failed to watch every step, a crevasse could quickly claim his life. Failing to concentrate could lead to asphyxiation, freezing to death, or the death of a colleague.

When asked what he thought about while climbing, Hillary said he focused completely on the task at hand. Perhaps more than any other attribute, even physical strength and competence, mental clarity led to Hillary's success. He had to think clearly in order to make wise decisions. Hillary will forever be known as a man who could concentrate, focusing on the task at hand and setting distractions aside. His prize, at 11:30 in the morning on May 29, 1953, was becoming the first man to climb what was previously an unassailable mountain.

The story of Sir Edmund Hillary is a good illustration of our fifth week's task: giving up distractions to the dream. Specifically, we'll learn the importance not only of giving up distractions but of embracing the opposite—of focusing, paying attention, and setting our eyes and hearts on the goal of moving from mate to soul mate. You will learn, as I have, that becoming a soul mate requires singularity of purpose. You will learn, as I have, that this singular goal is well worth the price.

## Distractions

It should come as no surprise that the dream to become soul mates doesn't just happen. While nearly anyone can be a mate, it takes a special person—in fact a special couple—to be soul mates.

Just as Sir Edmund Hillary didn't wake up one day and decide to climb Mt. Everest, we cannot simply wake up one day and decide we'll live as soul mates. Just as Hillary had to prove and improve on his skills, we must do the same.

For you to discover that magical place where you anticipate your mate's needs, relish his or her company, and consider loving your spouse a privilege, you must rid yourself of distractions. Becoming soul mates requires singularity of purpose and a commitment to do some "housecleaning" in yourselves—to identify and sweep away any diversions from your quest.

Let's reflect upon some distractions to the pursuit of being a soul mate.

*Lack of inspiration.* Believe it or not, some people simply don't think about being a soul mate. Lacking inspiration, they fall into a mediocre marriage much like one settles into a long-term, uninspiring job.

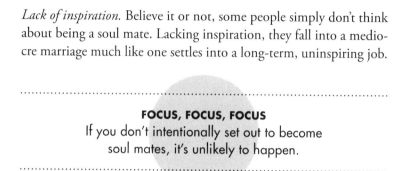

**FOCUS, FOCUS, FOCUS**
If you don't intentionally set out to become
soul mates, it's unlikely to happen.

Sure, they show up every day. They persevere. But there is no fire in their bellies or songs in their hearts.

In his book *Finding Ever After*, Robert Paul explains the importance of inspiration. "Without inspiration, we do not grow. When we originally took hold of our dreams—for life, for marriage, for ever—deep inside us was a divinely placed longing to be dynamic (not static), active (not passive), changing (not stagnant). We were made to be energized and vital. In a word, God created us with the desire, the passion, to be inspired."[1]

Unfortunately, too many couples accept mediocrity. They lose the vision for a vital and energized marriage. Soul mates, on the other hand, know how to maintain vitality in their marriage and will settle for nothing less.

*Lack of vision.* Closely related to a lack of inspiration is a lack of vision. Hopefully by now you realize that there is a vast difference between a marriage and a soul-mate marriage. Until you do, you're not likely to push for more.

How can you develop vision if you never had it? How can you imagine greater possibilities if you have settled for a lot less for a long time? The answer, I believe, lies within you. Solomon said, "He has planted eternity in the human heart" (Ecclesiastes 3:11, NLT). God placed in our hearts the desire for what he desires—and God desires that our marriages be places of abundance.

Frances G. Wickes tells the story of finding a Ming temple painting in a junk shop. He took it home and sent for an Asian man who restored such treasures. The man stood before it a long time and finally said, "Yes, I will fix it. I will take it now." When asked how long it would take, the man said he didn't know. When asked what it would cost, he said he didn't know that either.

After several months, the man returned with the restored painting. Impressed, Wickes said, "No wonder it took so long."

"Not the work," the man answered. "That was swift; but the vision. I go into the country. I sit all day under a tree. It does not appear inside me. I am too far away. I may go again and again. One day I see it. Then I work swiftly."[2]

Apparently the work was easy—capturing the vision was more difficult. Such is the case for many couples seeking to improve their marriages. While you might be distracted by mediocrity and tempted to settle for less, God wants more for you and your mate. You and your spouse must take time to develop the vision for your marriage, which will set the tone and direction for becoming soul mates. This vision is an image, or set of images, you hold in your mind, which creates positive feelings and actions.

Do you have a vision for something more in your relationship? If not, how might you create a new vision? An easy way to begin is to watch other couples in love and determine to incorporate some of those actions and attitudes into your marriage. Just last evening my wife and I walked by a young couple sitting on a park bench, holding hands. I was reminded of how much I enjoy it when Christie reaches out for my hand. A few yards farther, we saw another couple giggling as they shared a story, reminding me of the importance of sharing laughter and memories. Examples for creating a vision for your marriage are all around.

*Passing pleasures.* The pull is incredible. Can you feel it? There is an undeniable pull away from your marriage and your mate. There will always be something pleasurable ready to pull you out of the orbit of serving and loving your spouse. Whether it is the lure of television or the pleasure of eating, sleeping, or even exercising, anything can become desirable and pull you away from keeping your mate in the front of your mind.

Once you have settled for a ho-hum relationship, you will be more prone to seek pleasure outside of your marriage. Is your marriage one of function or friendship? Is it task oriented or a place of exquisite pleasure? If your marriage is mediocre, you'll be tempted to look for pleasure elsewhere.

Do you still find pleasure in your mate? When you think about him or her, do you feel a strong connection? The pleasure you find in other activities or things can be found once again in your mate.

*Detachment.* It takes energy to attach ourselves to someone. But it's easy to detach, to give up caring. It takes little effort and can be so very tempting to give up on your marriage, or at least on hav-

......................................................................................

### DIVE IN, DON'T DRIFT
Becoming soul mates takes effort. As soon as you see yourself beginning to detach from your mate—whether out of anger or boredom—consciously move toward your him or her.

......................................................................................

ing a soul-mate marriage. Many people are care-less. They have few meaningful attachments, feel little passion, and seem to drift through life. Attachment to our mates and the energy to insist on becoming soul mates requires effort. Notice when you begin to detach and guard against it. Make the unspoken spoken. Speak up and speak out instead of withdrawing.

*Attachment.* While detachment is easy, attaching ourselves to things that make no demands in return also requires little effort. Without thought, we attach ourselves to things that mesmerize us—the Internet, television, even busyness. We live cluttered lives and then suffocate beneath it all. We seem oblivious to the amount of stuff we bury ourselves with those things that distract us from being soul mates.

Adele Ahlberg Calhoun, author of *Spiritual Disciplines Handbook*, notes that "we remain blind to our attachments. . . . We ignore our fixed attachment to our identity and how it is represented in our drive for possessions, control, comforts and achievements. We avoid any mini-death of relinquishment we possibly can."[3]

I'm embarrassed by my attachments. It is only after I come back from visiting a poorer nation that I realize just how much stuff I've collected. I tend to "live to work" so I can have more things, rather than "work to live" so I can enjoy what I have. While I like to think I can live with little, the risk of doing so causes me to pause and reconsider. Most of my attachments, unfortunately, get in the way of truly attaching effectively to the people who mean the most to me.

Consider your attachments. What activities receive your attention? What objects receive your admiration? Where do you spend your energies? It may be time to shift your attention back to your mate, focusing on becoming soul mates.

*Procrastination. I'll do it later*, you tell yourself, though, of course, later never comes. We promise ourselves we'll find time in the future, only to find that the future never arrives.

We cannot afford to wait until later to attend to our marriages, any more than we can afford to neglect our health or finances until later. We cannot afford to give our mates the attention they deserve later, for later will be too late. If we wait to improve our marriages, we'll lose the opportunity to transition from mates into soul mates.

The time to make changes in your marriage, of course, is now. Today is the time to dedicate yourself to being the best mate you can possibly be, to go after the best your marriage can be.

*Half measures.* The Twelve Step program of Alcoholics Anonymous tells us that half measures do little for us. Certainly we can't expect to give half efforts and reap soul-mate results.

I'm reminded of this tendency in myself. It's especially tempting when it comes to household projects, which I dislike. Whether it's mowing the lawn, trimming the hedges, or cleaning our basement, I often offer half measures. The results show it.

I'm not proud of this tendency and have given these tasks more of my energy in recent years. Why? Because I want our home to be something we can take pride in. I want people to notice a well-kept house when they come to visit. Most important, my wife values these things, and my efforts show that I value her.

There is another reason for giving our best efforts to our homes and marriages. God expects excellence from us. Paul in his letter to the church at Corinth speaks about excellence: "You excel in so many ways—in your faith, your gifted speakers, your knowledge, your enthusiasm, and your love from us" (2 Corinthians 8:7, NLT). Clearly excellence is the expectation.

*Trapped by the urgent.* There is always something needing to be done. We all have a laundry list of unfinished tasks, issues requiring immediate attention, and people needing our care. Are these issues important? Undoubtedly. Are they as important as we make them? Not likely.

My days are always full. My wife likes to say that as soon as something is cleared off my plate (or before), I've already added something else to it. I wouldn't know what to do with myself if I wasn't tending to something I deemed urgent.

But this busyness, this sense of inflated self-importance, can be a distraction to more important things in life. If I'm not extremely careful, these seemingly important matters can edge out the truly important matters of the heart. If I'm not watchful and perhaps even a bit wary, I get caught in the tyranny of the urgent. Before I know it, I've solved other people's critical problems but am left with a mess of my own.

*Discouragement.* The final distraction to the dream of soul-mate living is the emotion and mood of discouragement. Discouragement, which is the polar opposite of encouragement, is a primary robber of joy. Discouragement occurs when someone has reached his or her limit, convinced that life cannot possibly improve.

Discouragement says, "Why try to have a soul mate when you're hardly able to keep a mate?" Discouragement says, "Why try to dream big? Dreaming small hasn't gotten you anywhere." And so, in a mood of profound discouragement and despair, we give up our dream. Discouragement robs us of the hope of having more.

When we are discouraged, we forget that this feeling is only a temporary mood. Often it is even a distortion of reality. It is, in some respects, temporary insanity. The reality, after all, is that you can

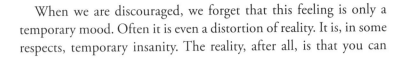

**DUMP DISCOURAGEMENT**
Don't let discouragement keep you down. Remember
that it is simply a mood—one that is temporary
and often reflects a distortion of reality.

make your marriage what you want to make it. The reality is that you can, using the tools offered in this book, move your marriage from mediocre to marvelous. There are no limits. You are limited only by the boundaries of your imagination.

## Focus

If distractions are the enemy of couples wanting to become soul mates, the remedy is found in focus. Laying distractions aside, refusing to be sidetracked by them, we choose to focus on having the best marriage possible. We won't settle for mediocrity. Our goal isn't to fix a bad marriage—we're intent on having a blissful marriage.

I'm reminded of a time in the mischievous days of my early adolescence when a couple of neighborhood buddies and I decided to play around with a magnifying glass and a bit of sunshine. You probably know what happened. A bit of sunlight strategically focused through a magnifying glass creates fire. Suddenly three boys were staring at burning grass, a light wind, and sparks flying in every direction.

Fortunately, among the three of us we had six feet to stomp the fire out with, but not before nearly having heart attacks. While we had hoped for a bit of heat, we hadn't anticipated a fire.

While spared the damage and danger of a large, blazing fire, I learned a powerful lesson about focus: concentrated energy can have a significant impact. Certainly this lesson is true in marriage as well, specifically when it comes to applying the principles discussed in this book.

Another way of explaining such concentrated intensity is what I call frontal lobe focus. The frontal lobe of the brain is largely responsible for executive planning. It helps us weed out extraneous material, focus on the topic at hand, create a plan, and then execute it.

Soul mates use frontal lobe focus. Soul mates practice:

- Keeping their mates in their minds throughout the day
- Thinking about what would please their mates
- Being considerate of their spouses, day in and day out
- Remembering special occasions
- Peppering their marriages with special events
- Knowing and living according to their mates' love language—those special things that say, "I love you!"

I have been asked if frontal lobe focus is sometimes a bit obsessive. Should we really have to think about our mates that often? Must we be preoccupied with our spouses? What about our individuality?

Yes, soul mates demand a lot of attention. Mediocre marriages are able to exist with a modicum of attention—soul-mate marriages cannot. Exceptional marriages require exceptional attention, concentration, and effort. But they are well worth the effort.

## Paying Attention

I love to tell the story about the time I received an important call while on the freeway. Without thinking, I frantically cupped my cell phone to my ear and tried scribbling something while nudging the steering wheel with my knees.

Within a few seconds, I knew I needed to pull the car to the side of the freeway.

No sooner had I pulled over when I noticed flashing lights in my rearview mirror.

"I'm in trouble now," I said feebly to my wife.

I rolled down the window to talk to the officer.

"Everything okay?" the officer asked.

"Well, yes," I said, still feeling anxious. "I just pulled over because

I received a call on my cell phone and realized I couldn't drive and concentrate on the call at the same time."

"I wish more people were as cautious as you," he said cheerfully. "Have a nice day."

With that I looked at my wife, dazed and delighted that not only had I avoided an accident, but a stiff ticket as well.

"You dodged a big bullet there," my wife noted.

"Indeed!"

Driving conditions, much like marriage, are not static. While long, straight stretches of highway in Montana may be rather mesmerizing, there are few "long, straight stretches of highway" in marriage where we can relax and give less than our full attention. Putting our brains on idle will never create and maintain a magical marriage. In fact, marriage demands our complete concentration. A marriage has the potential to be so dynamic that we must be alert at all times for changing conditions, including frantic cell phone calls.

There is a section of highway in Washington known for the number of accidents that occur there. Crossing over the Cascade Mountains in the winter on either Highway 2 or Highway 90 can be very dangerous. The problem isn't so much the ice and snow on the highways—though these elements add danger—it's unprepared motorists. Those who believe they can traverse this mountain range without studded snow tires or traction devices, some while talking on their cell phones, create incredible danger. The wise motorist packs chains, drives with studded snow tires, puts his cell phone away, and pays attention to changing road conditions.

Marriage is much like a treacherous mountain pass: it's filled with scenic beauty for those who pay attention but it's also peppered with road hazards. Those who take marriage for granted, assuming they can safely navigate changing conditions, will find danger lurking everywhere.

"I want you to pay more attention to me," Gail said emphatically to her husband, Kyle, in a recent marriage session. "You spend time fixing up your race car and buying the latest stereo equipment, but you haven't noticed what's happening to our marriage."

"What's that?" Kyle asked innocently. He looked at her, awaiting her response.

"You don't notice," Gail said. "You haven't noticed that I've grown more upset in recent months. I've been wanting to take a vacation so we can spend some uninterrupted time together, but each time I bring it up you offer some reason why we can't take one."

An attractive woman with piercing brown eyes, Gail had brought this topic up before in our counseling sessions. She was no longer

### ACT NOW, DON'T WAIT

The infomercials get one thing right—sometimes you can't afford to wait. That's certainly true with your marriage: if you aren't taking action to strengthen it, it will get weaker and weaker.

content to have "an average marriage." She wanted more but felt she wasn't able to get Kyle's attention. She felt misunderstood and sensed his lack of interest. He didn't seem to understand that their marriage was changing. The energies he gave to the marriage previously weren't enough now.

"You can't just run on automatic pilot," Gail said, obviously annoyed. "I want to feel like you're always interested in me. I want to feel that you're paying attention to how we're doing."

"I do, dear," Kyle said sincerely. "I am paying attention. You don't notice how often I listen to you?"

"It's not enough," Gail said, pausing to look over at me. "Is it just women who want their husbands not to be distracted? Is it just women who want their husbands to be tuned in to them, all the time? I feel so selfish asking for so much, but it's what I want. I need Kyle more at some times than at others, *and I want him to notice when I need him more!*"

"What do you think, Kyle?" I asked.

"She's got a point, and no, I don't think it's too much to ask. It's going to take a lot of energy. It's going to take focus and learning to read her. I'd like to try, but she's going to need to be patient with me."

"I can do that," Gail said softly. "Just saying you'll really try, watching for changes in me, makes a lot of difference. If you'll try, it really shows me how much you love me. You can't just love me and then set me on a shelf."

"What else can I do?" Kyle asked.

"I've been saying I want to put money aside for travel," Gail said. "I think that would be good for our relationship. It is important to me because it will help build an 'us.'"

Kyle seemed to understand the importance of this issue, emphasizing that he really loved Gail and wanted her to be happy. Still, it was a challenge to learn to watch and pay attention to her changing moods, her changing needs, and her changing expectations. Automatic pilot never works in a relationship, especially between soul mates.

## Attunement

The opposite of distractions may be attunement, or awakening. Distractions in marriage, of course, lead us to something like sleepwalking. We go through the motions, but we're not really attached or tuned in to our mates. We offer some attention, much like Kyle did for Gail, but there is no emotional attunement—no continual sensitivity to what is occurring in the person and relationship.

When we awaken and tune in to our mates, we stop talking on our cell phones, quit multitasking, give up distractions, and engage in frontal lobe focus, paying attention to what is happening with our mates and our marriages *this very moment*.

Getting stuck in old patterns of behavior puts us to sleep. While at some level we may know our marriages are not as fulfilling as they could be, we stop paying attention. We don't take the time to really become attuned to the state of our marriages at every moment. We're operating on an unconscious level of mindlessness.

In his book *Love's Journey*, Michael Gurian tells stories of many individuals and couples who have awakened and learned to effectively tune in to one another. Before people can effectively connect with another individual, he says, they have to learn to tune in to themselves effectively. If an individual is sleepwalking through life, he or she will never be able to truly tune in to his or her mate.[4]

Not long ago I worked with Kyle individually. It was shortly after Kyle had forgotten their wedding anniversary. Gail was particularly frustrated and hurt, since she and Kyle had spent much of their time in counseling learning the importance of tuning in to each other's needs.

"I'm not sure how I could have forgotten our anniversary," Kyle said with frustration. "I know better. I want to impress Gail, and here I go and do something dumb like that."

"How do you think it happened?" I asked.

"I didn't put it in my planner. I thought I would just remember, and obviously that didn't work."

A bit surprised, I pressed further.

"You didn't make yourself any notes or plan ahead?"

"Nope. Pretty dumb, I know. I think that is a pattern for me, I get so distracted doing the things I do every day, and Gail gets what's left over. It's got to change."

"How is Gail feeling?" I asked.

"She's hurt but knows I'm here talking to you. She understands I want to get better at waking up and taking care of business. I really am serious about improving our marriage."

It was not enough for Kyle to promise to do better. He had done that before. He was already a "good man," but now he needed to become attuned to Gail. He also needed to tune in to himself. He needed to pay attention to his own feelings and thoughts throughout the day. He needed to practice listening regularly to his own feelings of disappointment, sadness, and fear. As he becomes acquainted with his own feelings, he will more easily notice them in his wife.

Listening to himself was as difficult for Kyle as listening to his wife. I wasn't surprised. Since he hadn't known how to recognize the nuances of his own feelings, he had been unable to recognize them in his mate. As he learned to feel the subtle changes within, he needed to pay attention on a daily basis to the subtleties in Gail and in their marriage. Once he became attuned to the smallest changes in his wife and in their marriage, he would no longer forget the bigger things, like anniversaries.

Perhaps the perfect example of attunement is the relationship of a mother to a newborn child. My daughter-in-law, Jacqueline, is never far from baby Caleb's sight. She has tuned in to his particular whimpers and cries, distinguishing "I'm hungry" from "I need attention."

She knows when he is sleeping and when he is awake. She listens with *receptivity*.

What would happen if we listened receptively to our mates? We would listen with the anticipation of meeting a need. We would listen expecting to learn something new. We would be ready to be influenced by our mate. We'd be open to changing, willing to practice the new skills necessary to be a soul mate.

Can you understand the importance of attunement? Can you sense how it pulls us out of our solo orbits and into the orbit of our mates?

## To Love and to Cherish

Committing ourselves to remaining in sync with our partners demonstrates not only that we are attuned with our spouses, but that we cherish them. In *The Road Less Traveled*, Scott Peck tells us that truly loving another person means extending ourselves for the other's well-being.[5] The apostle Paul tells us that love is giving, not self-seeking nor insistent on its own way. In 1 Corinthians 13 we learn about the importance of cherishing our mates.

But what does it really mean to cherish someone? In 1 Corinthians 13:7, we read four important truths necessary for loving and cherishing our mate: *love protects, trusts, hopes, and perseveres.* During months of counseling, Gail and Kyle practiced applying these truths to their marriage.

*Cherishing protects.* Kyle learned the importance of protecting Gail's feelings. He learned the value of letting Gail know he was listening and that she could depend on him to be aware of her needs. She wanted him to sense when she was in a bad mood and offer to talk without her always having to ask for his attention. She wanted to know that he cared enough about their marriage to guard against being interested in other women and to let her know he wanted her affections completely for himself.

*Cherishing trusts.* Both Gail and Kyle wanted a marriage in which they could trust each other. They wanted to know they would be faithful and could count on each other to be available emotionally, spiritually, and physically. They worked on creating a relationship in which they felt safe when bringing any problem to the other, including their concerns about each other.

*Cherishing hopes.* Gail and Kyle wanted a marriage that was filled with hope and possibility. They worked on creating a relationship that was positive, encouraging, and fun. While they built on their past, they dreamed into their future. Kyle intentionally encouraged Gail in her desires to travel and learn Spanish. She intentionally encouraged Kyle's desire to become an entrepreneur, expressing her willingness to take a few more risks in their lives.

*Cherishing perseveres.* Gail and Kyle made it clear to one another that they would always be there, in good times and in the more difficult times. They agreed that nothing would pull them out of the marriage, which allowed them to feel safe. They vowed to listen to each other's dreams and help each other fulfill them. They had created many wonderful memories in the past and dedicated themselves to creating even more in the future.

Reflect upon how much you care for your mate. Consider his or her value to you. We cherish those people we value. We dedicate ourselves to meeting their needs. We know what makes them feel good and set out to create an environment in which they will thrive and prosper. This is the essence of cherishing another person.

## Eyeing the Prize

What is your number one goal in life? Maybe it's to send your kids to college or to build a retirement account. Maybe you're determined to raise godly children. Maybe you want to climb the corporate ladder of success.

Having goals is a good thing, because without goals you will be without focus—and we've already determined that focus is critical to being soul mates. Focusing on things other than what is critically important to you and your values can lead you astray.

Jesus is our supreme example of how to reach our goals. We read the following in the Gospel of Luke: "As the time approached for him to be taken up to heaven, Jesus resolutely set out for Jerusalem" (Luke 9:51).

Jerusalem was the place where Jesus' life and ministry would be fulfilled. His entire purpose on earth was to save lives through his life and death. The Cross was set before him, and he knew his time on earth was coming to a close. With his eyes passionately set on the prize, he would allow nothing to distract him from his purpose and mission.

This week's challenge has been to give up all distractions to your dream. Your task is to get rid of anything that distracts you from that prize. Clarity of purpose has always been the path to achieve one's vision. Focus, intention, and determination are the keys to victory. When you keep your eyes passionately on the prize—becoming a soul mate to your mate—you will not be disappointed.

## Weekly Quiz

Soul-mate relating requires focus and giving up distractions. To create this kind of vibrant and exciting relationship, you must set aside other concerns that seem to demand your attention so that you can make your marriage central in your life.

Consider this scenario:

You've had a tough week and are looking forward to relaxing over the weekend. Your mate, however, wants to "get out" and do something new and exciting. You

a) complain about being tired and discourage any activities, settling into another mundane weekend instead.

b) sense the importance of meeting your mate's needs and explore possibilities. Together you agree to relax for part of the weekend and try something new on one of the weekend evenings.

## PUTTING IT INTO PRACTICE THIS WEEK

1. Are any distractions robbing your marriage of vitality and meaning? If so, what are they?

2. Talk with your spouse about any "housecleaning" you need to do in yourselves. Identify those diversions you need to sweep away to get back to the business of building your marriage.

3. With all of life's busyness, it may take effort to keep your spouse in the front of your mind and to think positively about him or her. Which of the following will you begin doing to make that happen? As you decide, consider which of these might mean the most to your spouse.

   - Call your spouse midday just to say you're thinking about him or her

   - Make a point to thank God each day for your spouse and ask him to bless his or her day

   - Before accepting an invitation, take a minute to discuss it with your spouse

   - Surprise your mate with a bouquet of flowers or an encouraging note

   - Plan a special evening on your anniversary or your spouse's birthday

# EMBRACING THE RIPPLE EFFECT

*If you're going to be thinking, you might as well think big.*
—Donald Trump

**SIGNS THAT YOU NEED TO EMBRACE THE RIPPLE EFFECT**
**1.** You agree that just a little more effort could make a big difference in your marriage—and wonder why your spouse isn't making it.
**2.** The last time you spread any buzz about your spouse, it was to complain to your friends about his or her latest irritating habit.
**3.** You often find yourself on the defensive when talking with your mate.
**4.** The only "Zest" left in your house is the bar of soap in your bathtub.
**5.** You'd much rather tune in to tonight's episode of *CSI* than tune in to your spouse.

In the business world, exciting ideas are called "buzz," and the people who spread the buzz are called "sneezers." According to buzz-mogul Seth Godin, author of *Purple Cow*, "Sneezers are the key spreading agents of an ideavirus. These are the experts who tell all their colleagues or friends or admirers about a new product or service on which they are a perceived authority. . . . Best of all, . . . a few sneezers can get you to the critical mass you need to create an ideavirus."[1]

Now perhaps you're new enough to these concepts and words that you're asking yourself, *What is an ideavirus, and what does it have to do with being a soul mate?*

I'm glad you asked.

According to Godin and other marketing mavericks, an ideavirus is an idea that creates excitement, or buzz, and then multiplies as it spreads. It is passed on by way of sneezers who fall so in love with an idea that they spread the word for free. (If, at this point, you're thinking about the spread of the gospel, yes, this would be an ideavirus whose time had come during Jesus' ministry and whose messengers couldn't keep their mouths closed.

Because I'm interested in marketing, as well as in helping couples become soul mates, it occurred to me that the very same buzz used to create ideaviruses could be used to bring out the best in your mate. Why not? If we can create buzz about Starbucks coffee, Mont Blanc pens, Krispy Kreme donuts, and BMWs, can't we stir up enthusiasm and inspiration in and about our mates? And if we can stir up some enthusiasm in and about our mates, can we stir up some enthusiasm in and about ourselves as well? Of course we can!

We can spread the word, again and again, with the same type of "contagiousness" as a virus, so that the word circulates, resonates, excites, and continues the positive vibe. We can take what we've learned in previous chapters about focus and intentionality, and by adding positive energy, we can create and sustain positive feelings.

This leads us to our sixth task in moving from mates to soul mates: embracing the ripple effect. In short, the ripple effect has to do with you speaking positively about your mate, while he or she speaks positively about you. You notice the best in your mate, and he or she notices the best in you. Put into practice again and again, this rippling of positivity will transform your marriage.

## Tipping Point

I'm practically giddy as I write this chapter. Why? Because I believe I've discovered something powerful, an idea worthy of being an ideavirus. I believe if I can get enough people to start noticing the strengths in their mates and speaking positively about them, we might even start a movement. Not only will you embrace the positive effect of bringing out the best in your mate, but you'll become a sneezer, creating buzz, leading to a virus (an abundance of positive feelings), ultimately reaching a tipping point where talking positively about your mate becomes perfectly natural—and he or she will be doing the same for you.

Okay, I'm getting a little ahead of myself. I'll slow down.

Several years ago Malcolm Gladwell wrote a book that created quite a stir (buzz!), titled *The Tipping Point*. The premise of his book was that little things *can* create a huge difference. At some time, perhaps when we least expect it, small changes can ripple outward until a critical mass or "tipping point" is reached.

Gladwell opens the book telling the story of Hush Puppies, a brand of shoes that had been all but dead for years. Sales had declined to practically nothing. And then something strange happened.

Two executives ran into a stylist in New York who shared that classic Hush Puppies had suddenly become hip in the clubs of downtown Manhattan. People were going to resale stores and buying up the shoes. And then it happened: between 1994 and 1995 the market for Hush Puppies skyrocketed. Designers started calling the company asking for the shoes. In 1995, the company sold 430,000 pairs, up from 30,000 pairs a year earlier.

How did this happen? "The shoes were an incidental touch. No one was trying to make Hush Puppies a trend. Yet, somehow, that's exactly what happened. The shoes passed a certain point in popularity and they tipped."[2]

Gladwell continues giving examples of his theory—how little things can make a difference. How one act, built upon another act, can create energy and excitement. He reminds us of the 80/20 Principle, the concept where in any situation roughly 80 percent of the work will be done by 20 percent of the people. For the sake of our discussion, we can say it doesn't take much energy to create buzz. A little effort goes a long way. A few people really can make a dramatic difference—or, applied to your marriage, a little positive effort can have a profound impact.

## Ripple Effect

Influenced by the ideas of buzz, sneezers, and ideavirus, as well as the notion of "the tipping point," I suddenly wondered why these ideas couldn't be applied to couples, especially those intent on creating more excitement and enthusiasm for their marriages. These principles, I decided, were perfect for those wanting to move from mates to soul mates by generating the ripple effect. But what exactly is the ripple effect?

The ripple effect is simply this: when you notice and comment on the wonderful traits in your mate, and he or she notices and comments on the wonderful traits in you, positive qualities as well as positive feelings reverberate in your relationship. When a wife is feeling prized and admired, secure in her husband's love, she wants to encourage him. When a husband feels appreciated and encouraged, he wants to meet his wife's emotional, spiritual, and physical needs. And the positive vibe continues, nearly effortlessly.

Now remember what we learned about ideaviruses. These positive vibrations don't stop. They don't run out of gas. Soul mates bask in the positive energy permeating their relationship. No one suffers

........................................................................................

### CHAIN REACTION
One small, positive action in your relationship,
followed by another and another, will dramatically
improve your feelings toward one another.

........................................................................................

for lack of encouragement. No one suffocates for lack of emotional oxygen. There is plenty of delight and wonder to go around. The encouragement and excitement continue.

I'm sitting in a local bookstore as I write this chapter. Christie is sitting across from me, editing my last three chapters. I occasionally reach out and touch her hand, thanking her for her tedious efforts. She smiles back at me and blows me a kiss, which makes me jump up and give her a big hug. She is slightly embarrassed but pleased by my spontaneous action. This is the ripple effect in action.

Touching her hand is such a small action. Insignificant really. But I know these small gestures are the things that warm her heart. When her heart is warm toward me—which, thankfully, is most of the time—she makes small but meaningful gestures toward me. One small gesture, built upon another, reverberates and creates a tipping point in our marriage. Slowly, almost insidiously, Christie and I move from mates to soul mates. We feel each other's feelings, notice each other's moods, catch each other's eyes. We finish sentences in unison.

Together we create a ripple effect of warmth, affection, and generosity that goes on and on and on.

I'm hoping you'll help me get the word out: each of us has the power to positively influence our mates, bringing out the best in him or her and setting our marriages on fire. One small match is ignited, and the blaze begins.

Lighting a match, of course, results in an explosion of energy that creates even more energy in the form of fire. Fire can be either positive or negative, much like power and influence. While we often think of power and influence in negative terms, fearing someone may use them in manipulative ways, that is not what I'm talking about here.

What I'm talking about is the ability to use your personal, positive power to influence your mate and marriage for good. I want you to take your energy and use it to change your marriage from one of mediocrity to one of exceptionality.

Dr. Laura Schlessinger, in her book *The Proper Care and Feeding of Marriage*, emphasizes this point, noting that what we dwell upon in our marriages, what we think about day in and day out, is what is likely to come out of our mouths. If we want to create a positive virus, we must think about the positive attributes of our mates.

Schlessinger notes a concern about negativity being viral in marriage: "It is a fact that what comes out of your mouth is what sits on your brain. The more you talk to or about your spouse in angry, ugly ways, the more angry and ugly you are to them and feel about them."[3]

You have the ability to choose not only how you will view your mate but how you will treat him or her. You control how you think about your mate and what you will focus upon. You then choose what kind of comments you will make. In short, you have the power and influence to create a negative virus, or a positive one.

## An "Okay" Marriage

You might have already guessed that ripples of good feeling can be snuffed out quickly. Negative vibes can be started as easily, and perhaps even more so, than positive ones. Negative sneezers can ruin a day, stopping a positive movement in its tracks.

I worked with a man recently who had sneezing down to a science—

the only problem being he was a *negative* sneezer! It's not that Damon tried to be negative or was invested in remaining negative. He simply didn't know how to embrace a ripple effect. He knew nothing about buzz, good vibes, ideaviruses, or sneezers. Still, he could cause a dip in his wife's morale within fifteen seconds of walking in the door.

Damon was a thirty-year-old electrician who came to counseling with his wife, Marta. Dressed in his work shirt and ball cap, Damon slumped into one of my office chairs, betraying his cautious attitude. I felt a brief rush of energy leave the room.

Marta, too, seemed less than excited about being there. She offered a forced smile and said she thought that beginning counseling was a positive step in their relationship.

"Tell me what's brought you two to counseling," I said.

"You'll have to ask her," Damon answered, nodding toward his wife.

"Okay," I said brightly, trying to create some positive energy. I looked at Marta. "Why don't you tell me about coming to see me," I said.

"We have a good marriage," she reassured me. "I don't know that we need counseling. But I'm not sure that we don't either."

"So tell me why you made this appointment?"

"Kind of the typical thing," she said. "We've been married seven years, and it seems like we've hit a slump. End of the honeymoon and all that."

"Some of the spark seems to be gone?" I asked. "What do you think, Damon?"

Damon sat quietly, and then after a few moments he spoke. "I'm willing to be here," he said. "But I've got to tell you the truth. I have no problem with our relationship. I love Marta, and I know she loves me. I think her expectations are too high. She talks about stuff like 'soul mates,' and I'm not sure I think that's real."

"So you've got a good relationship, and it's good enough for you?"

"Yeah, I guess that says it. You know, I think in every marriage the woman always rates things lower than the man."

"That's probably true," Marta said, smiling and reaching out for Damon's hand. He smiled back at her.

"So different expectations," I said. "The marriage is good enough for you, but not for her."

Looking at Damon, I continued. "I'm assuming that Marta pushes for more and that you resist her when she does. Right?"

"I suppose that's the way it is," he said. "I wouldn't say I actively resist her. I just don't go along with all the things she wants to do. Guess that might not be the best thing to do?"

"Okay, let's get more specific," I said. "What things does Marta specifically ask for that you resist?"

Again, Damon took a few moments to reflect on their marriage. "She wants the mushy stuff women talk about," he said. "She wants hand-holding, candlelit dinners, me opening the door for her. It seems like a lot of effort for nothing."

"Oooh," I said. "Don't know if I'd say for nothing."

"I sure wouldn't," Marta said firmly. "This is exactly what I'm talking about. I try to create excitement in our marriage, but Damon acts like it's a waste of time. I know he appreciates nice dinners and romance, but he never seems to initiate it."

"Fair?" I asked Damon.

"Fair enough," he said. "So, Doc, do you think all these things women want are really necessary? Do you really need these things to have a good marriage?"

"I suspect you have many of the building blocks in your marriage: concern, safety, respect, stability, and a few other things. But without more, you won't be soul mates, which is what Marta wants. Like many women, Marta is saying life is too short not to have it all."

I asked Marta to share the impact of Damon resisting her efforts toward being soul mates. Becoming tearful, Marta began sharing even more openly.

"I love you, Damon. You are a very good man. I love so many things about you. We have two wonderful children. You work so hard for our family. You're a great dad. But I want a lot more positive things in our marriage. I want some adventure, excitement, passion. You know we had it once, and we can have it again. I need your help though. I can't do this alone."

"We had it once?" he said, almost surprised.

"You know you can dress up and make an evening of it for me when you want," Marta replied.

"I'm not convinced about all this," Damon said.

"Not convinced about what?" I asked.

"I just think that too many women want too much, and I'm not sure men have to give it. Those are my honest feelings."

Marta noticeably bristled.

"But I can see that it is really important to her. So I guess we'd better keep moving in that direction," Damon said. "It's been a while for me, so you're going to have to help me across the bridge. I've been a little stuck on one side for a long time."

With that we talked about their history and the excitement—buzz—they had had when they dated and during the early years of their marriage. We explored how Damon had created a great deal of excitement when he was dating Marta. I prodded him to remember daring actions he took to win Marta's affections. Damon sheepishly recalled dressing up as a bullfighter, greeting Marta at the door of her apartment with a rose in his mouth. He was willing then to take chances to win her affections—and needed to take some risks again to renew her affection.

Over the next several sessions, Damon seemed to soften, and his enthusiasm grew as he remembered how he had enjoyed and appreciated dating Marta. Full of compliments and encouragement, he had showered her with warmth and affection. We explored how to rekindle those emotions again and how to create a ripple effect.

## Creating the Ripple Effect

Damon wasn't as resistant as he first appeared. He wanted an exciting marriage and thoroughly enjoyed the times when he and Marta spent a weekend away at a bed-and-breakfast, leaving their children with her parents. He began to understand and embrace the notion of creating and perpetuating positive energy in a marriage.

As tough as Damon could be, he had a soft heart. He loved the attention Marta showered on him when they were away. He told her that he had secretly hoped she would be more loving toward him but hadn't known how to ask for it. I encouraged his honesty, explaining that communication, especially about spouses' desire for more intimacy and closeness, is difficult for most couples.

Marta was excited to hear Damon share from his heart. She felt encouraged to know that he really wanted many of the same things she wanted. Beneath his apparently indifferent exterior, he wanted warmth, affection, and intimacy.

Marta and Damon are like most couples. They were not in the habit of talking about intimacy. They hadn't considered the idea that one person could start a positive virus of affection and admira-

**MAKE WAVES**

When you comment on your spouse's positive qualities, and then he or she talks up your strengths, positive feelings will reverberate through your relationship.

tion that could continue on habitually. They didn't realize that with practice and reinforcement, these patterns could continue almost effortlessly.

Perhaps you're like Damon and Marta, out of the habit of talking honestly about intimacy. As I wrote about earlier in this book, intimacy is, frankly, "into me see." Begin one step at a time, sharing more and more honestly. Begin by revealing your personal feelings, asking for what you want and need. Ask your mate what he or she envisions for your marriage. Start the habit of sharing honestly.

## Negative Sneezers

Sometimes starting a positive virus is not as easy as it seemed to be with Damon and Marta. Spouses who are a little less willing than Damon can put out a fiery blaze with a sneeze—a negative sneeze, that is. There are people who, for a variety of reasons, have lost their passion. They are burned out and tired, having lost their zest for their mates. Sadly, these negative sneezers infect their spouses, causing pervasive negativity.

Negative sneezers abound. There are naysayers on every corner and in far too many marriages. If we are going to embrace the ripple effect, causing a positive stir in our marriages, we have some work to do. We must understand negative sneezers, identify what they do to snuff out positive excitement, and deal effectively with them. Negative sneezers have the following characteristics in common:

*They spread negative information.* Not only are they "dark-colored glasses" kinds of people, but they talk negatively. They "see" what's wrong in a relationship and talk about it incessantly. They grouse about what's happened in the past, refusing to move on.

*They rehearse trouble, and so trouble is the only thing on their minds.* Negative sneezers continue to harp on old news. They won't let the past go long enough to allow new experiences in. Convinced nothing will change, they are adept at making others feel just as discouraged as they feel.

*They refuse to try and embrace new experiences.* Negative sneezers won't try anything new because they choose to live in the past. They are stuck with the status quo, resisting new, adventuresome experiences. Rather than being open to new possibilities, they choose to review old experiences or simply live with the way things are.

*They try to convince you that things are as bad as they believe.* While you may feel optimism and possibility, if you listen to the negative sneezers for long, you'll be infected with negativity. You'll hear bad news, see and feel negativity, and before long you'll end up talking and feeling like they do.

Negative sneezers are stuck in a rut and want you to be stuck in the rut with them. Just as you have the power to influence your mate in positive ways, you also have the power to influence him or her in negative ways. You have the power to start a positive or negative virus. It is critical that you maintain your optimism, understanding that you alone choose your mood and emotional outlook.

## Stop the Infection

So how do you guard against being infected with negativity? To remain healthy, and to embrace the ripple effect, you must believe you have the power and influence to start a revolution of change in your marriage. It's okay to be the one to start the flow of positive energy with your optimism, compliments, bright outlook, and encouragement.

But wouldn't it be a lot easier if both mates were willing to embrace the ripple effect? Of course it would. This, however, may not be reality. Often one partner is more willing than the other to try new things, experiment with new possibilities, and spread the ideavirus of affection and love. Since you are the one reading this book, I appoint you as the person to start the virus. Will you embrace the ripple effect and start the process?

Assuming you answered yes, let me encourage you. There is nothing more addictive than positivity. There is nothing more inviting than someone with a cheerful countenance, ready to see new possibilities and willing to start over again in the face of disappointment.

Christie is the poster girl for embracing the ripple effect. She has an indomitably positive spirit. And it's contagious. It's like a virus, infecting me at the most surprising moments.

Several weeks ago I was in a foul mood, fighting a cold and feeling weary and dreary. I grumbled around our home one evening, letting Christie know I didn't feel well. I watched as she handled my negative sneezing with aplomb. Rather than being infected by my negative energy, she started a positive ripple effect.

"Honey," she said softly. "I know you don't feel well. You've had a tough day. Instead of us trying to stay up and becoming even more exhausted, why don't we go to bed early, read a magazine, and call it a night. I'll rub your feet for a few minutes, and you can take some cold medicine. That way you'll feel better, I get to spend some time with you, and we'll both get a good night's sleep."

Now you tell me—how could I stay cranky when faced with that proposition? Try as I might, I couldn't drag her down with me. Rather, she built a bridge to the benefit, taking a challenging evening and turning it into a more pleasant situation.

Do all of our interactions work that smoothly? Of course not. But Christie refuses to be infected by negative sneezing. Because she keeps her attitude's immune system in good shape, she rarely succumbs to negativity.

## Openness to New Ideas

One of the most powerful antidotes to negativity is being open to new ideas and possibilities. The ability to see opportunity in unlikely places is an incredible gift, but it's also a skill that can be learned.

Thankfully, Damon was open to experimenting with his world. He was willing to think differently, explore possibilities, and try new

........................................................................................

**IT'S ALL IN YOUR HEAD**
Make a point to think about the positive attributes of your spouse. When you do, the words you say without thinking are more likely to encourage than discourage him or her.

........................................................................................

things. I really appreciated his willingness, though I wasn't entirely surprised. After all, what did he stand to lose? Not much. What did he stand to gain? A lot.

In order for the ripple effect to take off, you must be open to new possibilities. You must be willing to open your eyes to adding new experiences to your love life. Opportunities are everywhere. Every friendship, travel experience, or evening out contains new possibilities for your relationship. Openness and flexibility is the key! Of course, these possibilities aren't that hard to imagine, and the benefit is obvious. Still, negative sneezers will find something wrong with any idea.

My wife and I recently returned from a vacation where we stayed in a bed-and-breakfast. Sitting at the breakfast table were three couples, all from different parts of the United States, all with different backgrounds and experiences. Each had different plans for the day. We listened intently as each couple shared where they had been, where they would be going, and what they would be doing. Some of their ideas sounded boring to us, while others sounded exciting. Christie and I took mental notes and altered our plans for the day based partly on the lively discussion at breakfast.

Consider how open you are to new ideas. Are you a believer or a doubter? Have you eliminated the word *impossible* from your vocabulary? According to Dr. David Schwartz, author of the best-selling book *The Magic of Thinking Big*, "'Average' people have always resented progress. Many voiced a protest toward the automobile on the grounds that nature meant for us to walk or use horses. The airplane seemed drastic to many. Man had no 'right' to enter the province reserved for birds. A lot of 'status-quo-ers' still insist that man has no business in space."[4]

Consider being flexible and remaining open to new ideas and perspectives mandatory for embracing the ripple effect. For the positive virus to keep moving, it needs an open and hospitable environment. It needs receptivity to new possibilities.

Take the following quiz:

1. Am I open to seeing things from a new perspective?
2. Am I willing to try new experiences in my marriage?
3. Am I willing to initiate new experiences?
4. Am I flexible enough to see my mate in new ways?
5. Am I flexible enough to behave in new ways?
6. Am I open to conveying positivity in my marriage?

Well, how did you do? Hopefully, you found that you are very willing to turn your marriage around by embracing the ripple effect. You also discovered, I hope, that you are willing to be the one to start the positive experiences, knowing that your mate will likely be infected by the powerful, positive bug.

## Bridge to the Benefit

As I've said, my wife, Christie, is the consummate builder of bridges to the benefit. That means she can infect positivity into any negative situation. She can find ways of making lemonade out of lemons. We all really need to learn this skill.

Just today she shared with me how she had gone into a shop and had a ticklish encounter. She told me about the following conversation she had had with the store's owner:

Shop owner: "Can I help you with anything?"

Christie: "No, I'm just wasting a few minutes of time waiting for my husband."

Shop owner: "You know, I think it's rude for you to tell me you're just wasting time in my shop. No store owner wants to hear that."

Christie took a moment to consider how she wanted to respond—not react!

Christie: "You're right, and I apologize. I can see why no store owner would want to hear that."

And with that Christie marched directly out of the store, right? Wrong. Christie engaged the shop owner in lively conversation, asking about her shop and its history. Christie asked to see some of her things and ended up walking out with a small gift for our family.

Don't be alarmed if you couldn't pull that one off the way Christie did. I couldn't, but I'm learning. Was the shop owner right in being so blunt with Christie? Perhaps not. But Christie turned a negative situation into something positive. Christie refused to be infected with the negative virus and instead decided to spread some of her good cheer.

Now let's consider how this might work in your marriage.

Your husband walks in the door and heads straight for the television without saying a word. You're tempted to say something sarcastic, which would cause him to say something snippy back before withdrawing.

...................................................................................................

**TALK ABOUT IT**
Most couples aren't in the habit of talking about intimacy.
But being open with your spouse about what each of
you needs from the other will bring you closer.

...................................................................................................

You'll both be losers in such an exchange.

Those who embrace the ripple effect will see every situation as a possibility for spreading the positive virus. It takes only a small amount of positive energy to ignite a blaze. You know you've reached a tipping point when the other person—your mate—begins to respond in kind.

So instead of being snippy, sarcastic, or rude, try the bridge to the benefit technique. What are you going to do in this situation? How about this?

Walking over to your spouse, you snuggle up next to him and

say, "I'd love to spend a couple of minutes with you before you get engrossed in a television program. How about if we talk about our day for a few minutes?"

Maybe you're more comfortable with a more direct approach.

"Honey, I'd really appreciate it if you'd spend a few minutes with me before you settle into watching television. Could we leave the TV off for an hour, or at least until after dinner?"

Maybe you want to be even bolder.

"You know what would make me feel great, and I'll bet you'd love it to? I know you're beat from your day, but I'd love the television to be off limits until we've had some time together. I want time with you and hope you want time with me."

In each scenario you've been clear about what you want. You've acknowledged your mate's need for relaxation and shown you are willing to negotiate with him. You haven't criticized him for turning on the television. See? Even a potentially tense situation has the possibility of starting the ripple effect.

## The Gift of Becoming One

The ripple effect of positivity, one person encouraging another, is more than just feel-good stuff. I'm not promoting ideavirus and the tipping point just because it feels good to bring out the best in your mate—even though it does!

I'm promoting it because God tells us it is our responsibility to do so. The apostle Paul makes our responsibility clear: "Keep out of debt altogether, except the perpetual debt of love which we owe to one another" (Romans 13:8, Phillips). Wow! We are to be engaged in the *perpetual* debt of loving one another. Not only is it our opportunity to love one another, but it is our obligation. We aren't given any options but to extend ourselves in love to each other. This means we don't stop when the going gets rough, but by God's grace we remain encouraged and press forward.

Damon and Marta caught the vision. While they are just beginning, they can see new possibilities. Even Damon, stuck for a long time in his old ways of thinking and being, was willing to embrace them. He promised to reserve one evening every weekend for an adventure with

Marta. He also agreed to prepare for the evening throughout the week so it would be an enjoyable experience for both of them. Marta was, of course, delighted and responded positively to his ideas.

If Damon can do it, so can you.

I'm promoting a new kind of thinking, and radical action, because I believe we are called to become one. God determined that marriage should be the place where two people become one flesh and live happily together in that physical, emotional, and spiritual situation. The Genesis account reflects the heart of God—that we should be united perfectly with our mates.

The ripple effect offers you and your mate the possibility of moving from simply being mates to becoming soul mates. This is an incredible gift. Rather than settling for living together in a mediocre marriage, I believe you and your mate can be soul mates, living blissfully together.

You may doubt your mate's willingness or ability to respond positively to your changes. Please keep in mind that positivity is contagious—it works. Even the most stubborn or detached mate will ultimately respond at least partially. While there may not be a radical transformation, everyone appreciates and responds to kindness, and in the process, you will be transformed!

You now have six powerful strategies for moving from mates to soul mates. In the next chapter you'll learn how to nurture your mate's dream, discovering its power to transform your marriage.

## Weekly Quiz

You're learning the power of the ripple effect. Positivity spreads quickly and creates a similar reaction in others. You must decide, however, to spread the good news.

Consider this situation:

Your marriage has become stale and you long for renewed energy and joy. You

    a) sit back and wait for your mate to become more exciting, only to be disappointed again and again.

b) decide to build positivity into your marriage, one step at time, by initiating simple, nonthreatening experiences that you both will enjoy.

.........................................................................................

## PUTTING IT INTO PRACTICE THIS WEEK

1. Make a point to encourage or praise your spouse at least once a day this week. Take note of his or her reaction. Do you see the ripple effect at work?

2. How open are you to new experiences and new ways of seeing things? If you haven't already done so, answer the questions on page 101 to find out.

3. If you are used to speaking critically or sarcastically, meditate on Ephesians 4:29 and Philippians 4:8. Ask the Holy Spirit to help you apply Paul's instructions in these verses.

4. Rather than reacting when you or your spouse is in a foul mood this week, take some time to think through and discuss the potential "bridge to the benefit."

# NURTURING YOUR MATE'S DREAMS

*Dream lofty dreams, and as you dream, so you shall become.*
*Your vision is the promise of what you shall one day be;*
*your ideal is the prophecy of what you shall at last unveil.*
—James Lane Allen

## SIGNS THAT YOU NEED TO NURTURE YOUR SPOUSE'S DREAMS

1. *Your* dream of owning a Nintendo Wii is brilliant and—let's face it—will probably come true on your next birthday. But your *spouse's* dream of buying a boat is ridiculous and impractical.
2. You'd like to connect with your mate, but you don't seem to have enough in common anymore.
3. The only dream you remember your spouse telling you about is how, as a four-year-old, he or she dreamed of becoming a horse. You think your mate might have been kidding, but you're not sure you want to broach that topic again.
4. You do know your spouse's dream—but are *reeeeallly* hoping he or she will just forget about it.
5. Your usual response when your spouse offers an idea is "That will never work."

It was hot and humid in our nation's capital on August 28, 1963, and tension was high. Our country languished in the throes of civil unrest. In the midst of this muggy melting pot, Martin Luther King rose to speak.

King was not just a leader. He was a spokesperson for those who felt it was taking far too long to put into motion the tenets of equality espoused by Abraham Lincoln; it was no accident that King's memorable "I Have a Dream" speech was delivered on the steps of the Lincoln Memorial. King spoke from Lincoln's platform, figuratively and literally.

In his profoundly moving speech that August day, King's passion for his cause was evident—that there would be a day when all people, regardless of race or creed, would be treated equally. Listening to King's historical speech, one gets a clear sense of his mission as well as his character: "I have a dream that my four little children will one day live in a nation where they will not be judged by the color of their skin but by the content of their character." Not only was King driven to deliver a message for his day but also for future generations.

Martin Luther King has always been a hero to me, not only for his courage in speaking an unpopular message, but for his tenacity and perseverance. During a recent visit to Atlanta, my wife and I slowly walked the streets where he and his family had lived, peering in the windows of the simple house he called home. We then made our way to the Ebenezer Baptist Church where his preaching began.

Listening to one of his speeches and walking through the Atlanta church where he and his father preached, I felt I gained a better sense of his passions, dreams, and character. I felt as though in some small way I knew him. In knowing what he cared about, in knowing what he died for, I knew him.

We can find a similar connection with our spouses by exploring and nurturing their dreams. Though their hopes may not be on so grand a scale as King's, knowing their dreams helps you and I understand what matters most to them. Perhaps the notion of nurturing your mate's dream is completely foreign to you. Let me assure you that this task is absolutely critical in connecting deeply with your spouse. As you come to know and nurture what is vital to your mate, you assist him or her in becoming all he or she and God desire. Your seventh task, then, in moving from mate to soul mate is nurturing the dreams of your mate.

I've known many people who could connect with their mates on an intellectual level. They clearly appreciate and respect one another. They are dedicated to each other and committed to their vows of faithfulness. They are close, share laughs and experiences, and enjoy raising their children and creating a lovely home together. Still, something is missing.

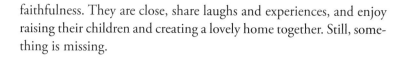

**PURE PASSION**
Discovering and encouraging your spouse's dream is a
surefire way to restore excitement to your marriage.

One of the primary differences between mates and soul mates is *passion*—pure, magical, mystical passion. Soul mates want to know what makes their mates' hearts beat. They want to know what their mates live for, perhaps what they might even die for. They want to know what brings a song to their mates' hearts. Sherry Suib Cohen sums up the benefits of understanding your mate's dreams: "Passion is empowering the other—then feeling stronger yourself."[1]

Dreams, very clearly, have power. They not only reveal our character, they drive us. Dreams are what make us get out of bed in the morning. They are the fuel that propels us forward when our bodies may be slow and stiff. Dreams are the passion causing us to care about someone, some thing, some purpose.

Any type of dream (even daydreams and nighttime dreams) carries with it something of importance. Each offers a message and is a harbinger of change.

A dream reveals much about the dreamer, his or her circumstances, and even events to come. While we may find ourselves "lost in our thoughts," the truth of the matter is that we're often not lost at all; in some regard, in such fanciful thinking we are "found." After all, we think and dream about what is important to us.

## The Keys to Nurturing Your Mate's Dream

### Listening

Not long ago I was home alone for the evening. Since we don't have a television and I didn't have music playing, the house was eerily quiet.

As soon as I settled into my easy chair, I began hearing so many creaks and groans, it was almost as if the house was talking to me.

*Was that a bird on the roof?* I asked myself. *No, it's too late for birds to be out.*

*Was that a raccoon rustling in the tree outside our door?*

*Is that the wind, or is it beginning to rain?*

Listening to the sounds of the night quickened my ears. In the quiet I was also able to hear myself think. Without the clamoring of demands, I was able to pay attention to my own thinking.

I was also able to think about Christie.

*What is she doing now?*

*When will she be home?*

*Is she having a good time?*

*Is she safe?*

Listening for your mate's dreams is like listening to the sounds in the night: at first you won't hear anything, but then as soon as you're very quiet, you hear *everything*. And since we're so often distracted by other demands on our time and attention, listening for your mate's dreams likely won't come naturally or easily.

Yet it really isn't that complicated once you know what you're listening for. Here are the questions I ask myself, and Christie, when listening for her dreams—dreams that create a special bridge between us when I understand and nurture what is critically important to her:

- What do you need?
- What is important to you?
- What do you want more than anything else in your life?
- What must happen to help you get it?
- How can I be helpful in nurturing your dreams?

## Showing empathy

Making a point to ask and then listen to our spouses' dreams is an important first step. There is something very powerful about sharing our dreams with each other. However, there is another step. The power and poignancy that can come when our mates share very personally will be lost unless we allow ourselves to be moved, even changed, by their dreams.

The process by which we are moved by our mates' dreams is called *empathy*, which occurs when we feel *with* someone—not to be confused with sympathy, where we feel *for* someone.

**GET INTO THEIR HEADS**
Spouses who ask questions and empathize with
their spouses' dreams are much more in tune
with their mates than those who don't.

Daniel Pink, in his fascinating book *A Whole New Mind: Moving from the Information Age to the Conceptual Age*, defines empathy this way: "Empathy is the ability to imagine yourself in someone else's position and to intuit what that person is feeling. It is the ability to stand in others' shoes, to see with their eyes, and to feel with their hearts. . . . Empathy is a stunning act of imaginative derring-do, the ultimate virtual reality—climbing into another's mind to experience the world from that person's perspective."[2]

What makes empathy so critical to becoming soul mates? Empathy is the ultimate act of attunement, when we focus completely on understanding our mates. We sense their excitement, feel their joy, strain to understand their vulnerabilities. It is the close connection the apostle Paul referred to when he said, "Rejoice with those who rejoice; mourn with those who mourn" (Romans 12:15).

I practiced this kind of listening with Christie recently. We were in the middle of preparing to sell a residence we had been renting out. We had decided to move back into that home so we could make repairs and paint it before putting it on the market. Christie took on the lion's share of the work, boxing our belongings, renting the U-Haul, and moving our things over to the house. She worked furiously for days, taking things to Goodwill, labeling boxes, and putting things in storage.

One evening I came home and found her quite dispirited. I asked how she was doing. She frowned and began to cry. I asked her the kind of questions I introduced on page 110. Her answers were direct, simple, and contained a theme I had heard long before this move.

"I want to be established," she said sadly. "I don't want to move anymore. I want a place of our own, where we can put down roots. I don't want to push for anything bigger or better. In fact, the simpler the better. Then when we are settled, I can decide what else I might want to do with my life. But not until then."

At first I had thought Christie's tears and sadness were simply a result of stress. Maybe she was just having a mini meltdown, the kind we all might have when overworked or overtired. Certainly she was overworked and stressed. But to play it all up to a "mood" would have missed the mark. By listening empathetically to her frustrations, I understood that her overwork had simply brought to the surface a dream she has for stability.

Accurately empathizing with Christie that evening brought healing and relief to her. Not only did I create a space for her to vent her feelings, but sharing her frustrations and dreams brought us closer. Empathy not only builds bridges between mates; *accurate empathy*—sensing your mate's feelings precisely—is a healing experience. When we fully understand our mates' feelings and they understand ours, healing occurs. It leads to a *corrective emotional experience* and builds an almost unbreakable bond between us.

## Noticing dreams and themes

As I listened to Christie that day, I knew she was *not* having a mini-meltdown. She was *not* having a panic attack or period of depression. She had *not* lost her mind—she had found it. The reason I knew this centers on the third key to encouraging our mates to share their dreams: picking up on themes that come up over and over. Christie was expressing a desire I had heard many times before: her desire for stability.

One of the most valuable aspects of our daydreams and musings is that the desires they reflect often center on the same theme. Because certain hopes are of utmost importance to us, they pop to the surface of our minds again and again. When we listen closely—and sometimes not so closely—we recognize the same theme.

As I listened to Christie that evening, it occurred to me she had been expressing the need for stability for months. There was no use in trying to offer her simple solutions, since there were none. It would have made no sense to try to dissuade her from her convictions, since she was expressing a core value. Her needs and desires were not going away, and my task was to embrace and empathize with them.

Another way of thinking about how to notice the themes of our spouses' dreams is to remember the childhood game of *connecting the dots*. The object is to connect a series of dots to reveal the shape of some mysterious object. The same exercise can be done with our mates, except in this case we connect words spoken over time and see what form they take.

In a moment of vulnerability, Christie shared her desire for stability. Had she been rested and relaxed, she might not have cried or expressed her desire the way she did. Still, the theme emerged. The dream had been there, inside her, ready and waiting for expression.

My task, as a soul mate, is to listen for themes like this in Christie's life. I want to listen to what she says and what she doesn't say. I want

---

**CONNECT THE DOTS**

Want to discover your spouse's dream? Begin listening carefully to the topics and themes he or she brings up again and again.

---

to listen to what she says, again and again, in different ways. I want to listen to what words, what expressions, come out over and over again. They reflect what is on her heart and mind. My ability to listen to her dreams and embrace them can be a powerful bridge to her.

But what if your mate's dream does not move you—or, worse, you think it is a clunker? The answer: Handle with care. Offer a tender ear and a strong dose of encouragement. Then listen for how your spouse's dream might be fulfilled, and offer possible assistance in achieving it. Dreams are special. Each is like a newborn child, needing a soft touch and gentleness. When your spouse shares his or her dreams, he or she is letting his or her heart become vulnerable. This is not a time for brutal truth, as much as you might want to offer it. This is not a time to dash hopes, crush wishes, or stall movement. Doing so guarantees tension and distance in a marriage, as Brian and Darlene discovered.

Before they arrived at my office the first time, I wondered why Brian and Darlene were coming to see me. While reviewing their intake chart, I noticed they had been married forty years. I wondered what a couple married that long might have to talk about.

Brian and Darlene had a marriage that had stood the test of time. Now residents of Washington State, they had spent most of their lives in Chicago, and I thought the bluntness of their speech reflected their ties to the Windy City. Both in their late sixties, they cared deeply about one another but were clearly fiercely independent.

"We're here because our lives have changed and he hasn't," Darlene said abruptly.

Brian didn't wince, though I did. I needed to respect this was the way they had communicated with each other their entire marriage.

"What do you mean?" I asked. "What exactly is the problem?"

"It's really hard to put into words," she continued. "Our kids are grown, and I've been restless for some time."

"Okay," I said, still wondering about the exact nature of their problem.

"What she's trying to say," Brian said, seeming annoyed, "is that she's wanted to move to Florida for the past five years and I don't."

"So you're not itching to go to Florida?" I asked Brian.

"Nope. Not Florida. Not Mexico. Not Texas. I don't know why anyone would want to go there."

"I want to go there," Darlene said firmly. "I've been saying I want to go somewhere warm for the past five, maybe ten, years. He just ignores me."

"I figure if I ignore her, maybe she'll let go of this crazy dream. But you can see where that's got me."

"Why do you think she wants to go to Florida, Brian?" I asked.

"Well, my first answer is that I don't have a clue. But that wouldn't be honest, because I really do have a clue. I just don't want to have a clue. Pretty stubborn, right?"

Brian smiled, obviously knowing that Darlene had dreams of warmer weather and he didn't. He hoped her dreams would die, but that wasn't happening. His denial of her dreams was taking a toll on their marriage.

"My desire to go someplace warmer is not going away, Brian," she told him. "You can ignore me, but I'm not going to shut up about it. And I'm starting to resent you for ignoring me. And neither one of us wants that to happen."

Brian eyed his wife of many years, offering a faint smile.

We spent the next several sessions talking about their dreams for their future. We talked about the power and importance of dreams and how they rarely die, at least not easily. We talked about how you can ignore someone's longings for only so long before they surface, in one form or another. We also talked about the missed opportunity when we fail to honor and respect one another's dreams, as different as they may be from our own.

## Be a Midwife to Your Spouse's Dream

While some men may react negatively to this image, I hope they see this example as simply another way they can help their mates fulfill their dreams. Brian and Darlene's story illustrates that it's not enough to listen to or even acknowledge our mates' dreams. Not only did Brian not want to help Darlene give birth to her dream, he hoped it would not come to fruition. He believed, at some level, that if he ignored Darlene's musings long enough, they would go away.

This was a big mistake. Dreams may simmer under the surface for years, but ignored dreams, dishonored and disrespected, create distance between mates. They can be like the proverbial elephant in the room.

Sadly, not only did Brian's egotistical behavior cause resentment, but he missed a golden opportunity to be a midwife to his wife's dreams. To hear her tell it, she'd been thinking about the Florida coast for years.

"We've gone to the Cocoa Beach area a couple of times over the years. The place has been untouched by time," she said excitedly. "The houses are still built of cinder blocks. They're low-slung, mid-century modern houses," she said, smiling. "They're just simple places. Bright colors. Lots of sunshine. And the beach. I could walk those beaches for hours and never get tired of them."

"You can help give birth to this dream," I told Brian. "Ignoring her won't make her dream go away. Why don't you explore possibilities with her? Listen to the excitement in her voice. She comes alive when she talks about those cinder-block houses. You can be part of that. You can help her find a way to accomplish her dreams."

What if her dreams conflict with his? What if the beach doesn't bring him the same pleasure it does for her? These are moments when compromise and creative discussion are appropriate. More often than not, however, when we fully enter into our mates' dreams, they become contagious. We start to share their passion.

Fortunately, Brian began to understand the damage his indifference to Darlene's dream was doing to their marriage. He listened and slowly warmed to my suggestion. He could see the truth of what I was saying. He began to consider how his world could be made larger—not smaller—by incorporating her dream. Doing so would rekindle a marriage growing cold from insidious resentment.

How about you? How are you doing at being a midwife to your mate's dreams? Consider these questions:

1. Do I know my mate's dreams? (We've all got them, even if at first we deny it.)
2. What has been my response to these dreams?
3. How would my mate like me to respond to his or her dreams?
4. Have I hindered my mate's dreams in any way?
5. What can I do now to become a midwife to his or her dreams?

Remember that it is just as important how you respond to your spouse's dreams as that you know what they are. In fact, soul mates are integrally involved in helping birth one another's dreams. In his book *Yearnings*, Rabbi Irwin Kula discusses the phases required to give birth to a dream or a new idea.

> *It's time to incubate, to allow those ideas to swim in our consciousness, to rub up against each other, even bang against each other occasionally. . . . We may come up against obstacles, both internally and externally: people who resist our ideas; ways we judge ourselves. We're doubting as much as we're discovering; eliminating as much as we're generating. We're struggling and wrestling with both new and old truths.*[3]

Can you see how important your role is? Given the fragility and the importance of dreams, our spouses often need help in turning their dreams into reality. A soul mate eases these transitions, encouraging the birth of a new idea. He or she willingly acts as a sounding board as a dream takes shape, offering encouragement and different perspectives.

So what are the keys to becoming a midwife to your spouse's dreams?

## Resonate with the dreams

Being a good midwife involves resonating with the dreams of your spouse. What do I mean by this? I mean that by active listening, by asking helpful and clarifying questions, you can encourage and reverberate with a dream. You can, with care and attention, literally *feel* the power of your spouse's dream. When you resonate with his or her plans, you share the excitement, acknowledge how each dream affects you and your mate, and help those dreams take shape.

For example, after watching and listening carefully to my wife throughout our marriage, I am aware of her passions.

She loves children's books.
She loves pugs.
She adores her children.
She prefers small, welcoming places, such as quaint towns,
    intimate bed and breakfasts, and cozy restaurants.
She loves to talk to strangers.
She delights in entertaining.
She is a romantic.
She loves the ocean.
She loves quiet and peacefulness.

These are the things that make her heart beat. When I attend to them, we are closer, emotionally connected. I can share facts and opinions, but when I meet her at one of these places of passion, there is an extra bit of energy. When I encourage Christie to share her feelings about these passions, she beams. When I make a point of noting her enthusiasm, she smiles. We meet at these places on a deeper level. When at the ocean, our hearts beat in unison. When we read a children's book at the ocean, with children playing nearby, there is magical passion. This is resonance at work.

### Create safety for the dreams

Remember that one of your tasks is to create a safe landing place for your mate's feelings. Intimacy—into-me-see—is based in large part on feeling safe with your mate. You have the opportunity to create a safe landing place for your mate's dreams.

Matthew Kelly, author of *The Seven Levels of Intimacy*, tells the story of a group of admiring college students who visited Beethoven's home in Bonn, Germany. One of the female students stared at the piano where Beethoven had written much of his famous music.

She asked a security guard if she could play it. Persuaded by a generous tip, he let her do so. Then she asked, "I suppose over the years all the great pianists that have come here have played the piano?"

"No, miss," the guard replied. "In fact, just two years ago I was standing in this very place when Paderewski [a celebrated Polish pianist and composer] visited the museum. He was accompanied by the director of the museum and the international press, who had all come in the hope that he would play the piano."

When offered the opportunity to play, his eyes welled with tears as he declined, saying he was not worthy even to touch the piano. Ironically, this master pianist saw what the guard and eager young student could not: Beethoven's piano is cordoned off from the public because it represents its original owner. It's of immense value today—an estimated 50 million dollars—because of our respect and reverence for Beethoven.

Kelly adds, "That is reverence, a deep respect that causes us to stop and look beyond appearances and discover a greater hidden value."[4]

Reverence. A deep respect that causes us to stop and look beyond hidden appearances. This conveys the attitude we must cultivate as we prepare ourselves to receive our mates' dreams. We must feel a profound respect for our mate. If we don't feel it, we must make a decision to cultivate it—now!

Consider for a moment the implications of disregarding your mate's dreams. Consider the impact of not respecting this most sensitive aspect of your mate's very personhood. To treat his or her dreams casually is to step right up to Beethoven's piano and play, without regard for the character of the composer.

If Beethoven is deserving of respect, what about a child of God—your mate? Listen to the words of the psalmist: "What is man that you are mindful of him, the son of man that you care for him? You made him a little lower than the heavenly beings and crowned him with glory and honor. You made him ruler over the works of your hands" (Psalm 8:4-6).

Your mate is loved and cared for by the Creator of the universe. Since the beginning of time your mate has been in the mind of God. In fact, we know that the dreams carried by your mate might very well be the dreams of the Creator himself. Does that cause you to pause? Making a safe place for your mate's dreams, and nurturing them, is your responsibility.

## Protect the dreams

What does this look like? Here are a few more ideas:

- *Create an ongoing Dream Incubator.* Yes, you can create an environment in your marriage where dreams are shared easily. When you show interest and enthusiasm, you make it easy for your spouse to share more about his or her ideas. When both mates see that dreams are tender forms of creativity that demand protection, they are much more likely to be vulnerable and open about their dreams.
- *Do not criticize your spouse's dreams.* Dreams need protection. Guard them. Don't criticize them and don't allow others to criticize them either.
- *Celebrate your spouse's dreams.* Find ways to encourage his or her dreams. Note what is good and exciting about these dreams. Talk about them and share the excitement. Find aspects of the dream you can resonate with.
- *Offer your mate your complete, undivided attention when his or her dreams are brought up.* Ask questions about his or her dreams. Be curious. Dare to dream deeper with your mate. What is the dream beneath each dream? What is the dream

beneath that? Your attention and questions will show respect, admiration, and reverence.

........................................................................................

**HANDLE WITH CARE**
Criticizing your spouse's dreams is like telling a mom
her baby is ugly—and just about as devastating.

........................................................................................

- *Dream for your mate.* When your spouse is discouraged, dream for him or her. Don't allow his or her dreams to be put aside. Encourage, amplify, and embellish the possibilities in your mate's dreams.
- *Accurately empathize with the passions and feelings of your mate.* Accurate empathy is powerful, as we've learned. It takes effort, however, to listen for the precise nuances of another's feelings. When you share your mate's feelings, sensing the value and importance of his or her dreams, a special bond is forged. The empathic connection is one of the strongest bonds available to us.
- *Be sensitive to your mate's shifting dreams.* Dreams, like the people who hold them, shift and change. A dear friend of mine spent fifty years building a television ministry with her life mate. One is a licensed professional counselor; the other a gifted and knowledgeable Bible teacher. They nurtured this ministry from simple roots to an expansive ministry by encouraging the dreams of the other. Recent health issues, however, have caused my friend to realize that she and her husband will need additional help in the years ahead. Though her vision, drive, and enthusiasm are as strong as ever, she says she is "listening to the Lord for new directions." This couple's story offers a helpful reminder: Our spouses' dreams are dynamic—they are rarely static over a lifetime. During one season we dream one thing, and at another time we dream something entirely different. Take special care to tune in to the various movements of your mate's dreams.

Have I convinced you of the importance of your spouse's dreams? Will you invite and protect the creative aspects in your mate? I hope so.

## A Powerful Dynamic

There is power, excitement, and incredible energy when spouses share the dreams of one another. Consider the possibility of discovering, encouraging, and sharing the dream of your mate. I call it "catching the dream."

Physicists are aware of a phenomenon of resonance called entrainment, the tendency for two oscillating bodies to lock into phase so they vibrate in harmony. A similar dynamic occurs when you are caught up in your spouse's dreams. It leads to the confluence of your mate's excitement with your own. Two separate people, because of shared dreams, have now become one.

Two people sharing the same dreams and the same emotions begin to think alike—soul mates! Two people who catch each other's dreams, who share the same excitement, who want the best for each other—soul mates! Two people who empathize with one another, feeling the feelings of the other, being on the exact same wavelength—again, soul mates!

Sounds a lot like the biblical account of two becoming one flesh, doesn't it? Instead of two separate people moving in distinctly different directions, we have an opportunity, by way of our dreams, to move in perfect harmony with each other. Will you nurture your mate's dreams? Will you add to his or her excitement? Don't miss out on this incredible opportunity to move from mates to soul mates.

In our next chapter, we'll explore how your mate can encourage and nurture *your* dreams, adding an additional element of excitement to your relationship.

## Weekly Quiz

This chapter was about nurturing your mate's dreams. Doing this takes special effort, but the payoffs are incredible. Joining your mate in his or her unique place of passion creates a special bond.

Consider how you might handle this situation:

Your mate wants to change careers, having grown tired of the job he or she has been doing for the past twenty years. You've known your spouse is unhappy, but obviously giving up the stability you've become dependent upon is frightening.

Observing your mate's growing dissatisfaction, you

a) avoid talking about it, since changing careers would require an uncomfortable time of transition.

b) encourage your spouse to explore making the change, allowing him or her to dream out loud and reassuring your mate you will do your part to ease the transition.

......................................................................................

## PUTTING IT INTO PRACTICE THIS WEEK

1. Make a point of listening for clues to your spouse's dreams this week. Does he or she frequently bring up the same topic? Does a particular song or movie seem to move him or her?

2. If you haven't already done so, take a minute to evaluate how well you're doing at being a midwife to your mate's dreams. To help you, answer these questions:

   • Do I know my mate's dreams? How would I summarize them?

   • What has been my response to my mate's dreams?

   • Have I hindered his or her dreams in any way?

   • In what ways might I help encourage my spouse or even help him or her fulfill a dream?

3. If your spouse in willing, talk about how you could make your relationship a "Dream Incubator." (See page 119.)

# TEACHING YOUR MATE TO NURTURE YOUR DREAMS

*If one advances confidently in the direction of one's dreams,*
*and endeavors to live the life which one has imagined, one will*
*meet with a success unexpected in common hours.*
—Henry David Thoreau

## SIGNS THAT YOU NEED TO NURTURE YOUR OWN DREAMS

1. *Dreams? What dreams? Who has time to dream?*
2. Whenever you go out for dinner with your spouse, you run out of things to talk about before the main course arrives.
3. You figure your dreams are so impractical that there's no point in dwelling on them.
4. The one time you tried to share your dream of writing a screenplay, your mate thought you were joking and burst out laughing.
5. You're happy to support your spouse's dream but aren't sure your longings are "good enough" to share in return.

Born in Concord, Massachusetts, to poor parents who made a living making pencils, Henry David Thoreau has been called "the first hippie." Though he was a Harvard-trained engineer, he decided early in life to move away from the crowds and live a solitary life.

In *Walden*, a record of his two-year stay at Walden Pond, Thoreau explains why he interrupted his busy life to withdraw from the world. "I went to the woods because I wished to live deliberately, to front only the essential facts of life, and see if I could not learn what it had to teach, and not, when I came to die, discover that I had not lived."

To live deliberately. Thoreau was intentional about his life. He wanted, first and foremost, to understand himself. While we may not agree with his lifestyle or his advocacy of civil disobedience, we can applaud his willingness to buck the trends of common pursuits of the day; namely to earn more money, advance in one's career, and rack up accomplishments. He wanted to live simply and be true to himself. This certainly is the stuff of dreams.

In addition to living deliberately, Thoreau espoused living as an individual. In another famous quote, Thoreau said, "If a man does not keep pace with his companions, perhaps it is because he hears a different drummer. Let him step to the music which he hears, however measured or far away."

The significance for us in Thoreau's work is this: we must allow ourselves to know and express our own dreams. After all, we cannot share a dream we have not embraced. We cannot share excitement about something that doesn't excite and invigorate us. We can't expect our mates to know our passion if we haven't felt it first. Knowing where our hearts beat leads to our eighth week's task and another way to build connection: *teaching your mate to nurture your dreams.*

While it is critical that you nurture your mate's dream, it is equally important to nurture your own dreams and to encourage your mate to learn to understand what touches your heart deeply. Your dreams, like those of your mate, are central to who you are and who you are becoming.

In the last chapter, we talked about the passions that dreams unleash in us. We often keep these passions hidden deep within. We know, intuitively, they are precious. We have so few of them and want to preserve them and keep them safe. At times, these passions are unknown even to us. Most times, however, we have clues, inklings about what makes us sing for joy.

I am a man of many dreams—at times, too many. I count on my wife, Christie, to help me explore them. This is a very sensitive task, as of course I want her to think every one of my ideas is fabulous. They're not. But when she listens carefully, she often resonates with them. Something in me resonates with something in her. This is soul-mate connection time.

Recently I talked to her about doing more public speaking. This wasn't a new thought, and she had heard me talk about this dream before. Wisely, she affirmed my dream. More important, she resonated

with it. Hearing about my dream of doing more public speaking reso-
nated with a dream inside of her to do more public speaking as well.
My excitement got her excited. Her excitement got me more excited.
Do you see how it can work?

## Know Your Dreams

When it comes to sharing dreams, we have a potential problem. We
cannot share what we do not know. We cannot teach our mates to
nurture our dreams if we are unsure about them ourselves.

Years of work, living outside ourselves rather than inside and close
to our inner nature, leaves many people feeling like strangers to their
own selves. We become so accustomed to meeting the external needs
of family, jobs, homes, and children that asking us to articulate our
dreams can leave us feeling stymied, puzzled, foggy.

If this describes you, you will need to awaken to your inner self.
You must attend to your soul and the work your soul is doing. You
must come alive to the passions that still flicker deep within.

This was true for Mark. When I began working with him and his
wife, Tricia, I quickly realized that one cause of the distance between

**GET PERSONAL**
Sharing your dreams with your spouse is
a powerful way to reconnect.

them was Mark's unwillingness to let his dreams and hopes surface.
It is a common practice of mine to encourage my patients to listen
to what they feel and want. Sometimes I have to ask them again
and again what is important to them. This was the case with Mark.
He had no ambitions for his marriage or his relationship with his
estranged wife.

Mark and Tricia had been married for twenty years but had been
separated for the last two. They came to me to see if their marriage
could be saved. Mark came willingly to counseling, though he was

very cautious. An astute businessman, he was more comfortable in the world of numbers than with people and emotions. He learned as a child that he was expected to do things perfectly, and thus he demanded perfection from himself as well as Tricia. He didn't like the sloppiness of emotions and relating.

Tricia was also a hardworking businessperson, but she more easily set aside her work in favor of relationships. She was able to share feelings and wanted a much stronger connection to Mark. Tired of living with Mark's criticism and scrutiny, she initiated their separation.

"Let's talk about what you both want," I said during our first session.

"I'm not sure," Mark responded. "I don't think about it all that often."

His response surprised me, though I meet many people who give surprisingly little attention to their inner lives.

"That's the problem," Tricia jumped in. "How can we ever get back together if he doesn't think about what he wants, or what I want?"

"Good question," I said, turning back to Mark. "You really have no idea what you want in your marriage?" I asked. "How has it felt to be separated for two years? Do you want to reconcile?"

"I'm not sure," he said again. "I suppose I should know, but I don't. When I think about getting back with Tricia, I feel confused. So I quit thinking about it."

"Let's go back and talk about what led to the separation," I said, hoping that reliving some of the past might help awaken the feelings leading to their separation. "Things weren't going well then, and some things need to change now for you both to want to be with each other."

I took Mark and Tricia's history carefully. Their stories revealed that their marriage had dissipated slowly but persistently as their careers had taken off. Time spent in their business pursuits, combined with that spent raising three children, had created a division between them. More important, they had stopped sharing their dreams and hearts' desires with one another. Communication had taken on a perfunctory quality—lifeless, hopeless, and lacking soul.

Working with Tricia and Mark was like shuffling through an old bookshop, discovering dusty, rare books. Peeling back layers of time and defenses, we explored who they were, who they had become, and what they needed from each other to become friends again.

"We used to be close friends, even soul mates," Tricia said nostalgically. "I loved Mark's abilities and keen intellect. We used to have long, deep discussions about world affairs. We'd spend hours talking about theology and laugh about funny things that happened during our day. I want to share that again with him. I want to learn again to talk and share stories. I want to dream with him. I don't want to feel like I don't measure up, which is why we separated."

"Do you know about his dreams, his passions?" I asked Tricia.

"Hmm," Tricia said slowly. "That's a good question. My first answer would be yes, but on second thought, I'm not sure I do. But I'd like to know."

"Does that sound inviting to you, Mark?" I asked. "Do you miss being friends with Tricia?"

I held my breath as he puzzled over his response.

"I think that would be nice," he said slowly. "But it's a stretch for me to think that way after being apart so long. There's a lot of distance between us. I'm used to meeting my own needs now."

"Yes, two years is a long time," I said, "and you've admitted there was tension before the separation. So it will take some work to build a bridge back to each other. But there's no reason it can't be done."

"I don't know what I want," Mark said again. "So it's tough to know how to proceed, and I know Tricia gets impatient with that answer."

"Well, you're here," I said. "I suggest we talk about the qualities you've enjoyed in the past with Tricia, and see if we can rebuild them. How does that sound to you?"

Mark nodded in agreement. Tricia looked at Mark and smiled.

As we talked, Mark discovered how he had pushed Tricia away. He discovered he didn't like conflict, and that even though he had been very critical of Tricia, he didn't like Tricia's criticism of him. He feared she would be critical again.

Over the weeks we found that both Mark and Tricia felt vulnerable with one another. They weren't sure how to manage critical feelings and certainly were not effective in sharing their needs. They began, slowly, to grow excited as they learned how to express their passions and desires. Gradually they became more open with each other, sharing more of their feelings and dreams.

## Passions of the Heart

Dreaming wasn't always easy for me, either. There was an extensive season in my life when I lived the opposite of what Thoreau advised—I was pressured, busy, tense, and sociable. I lived from the outside in, rather than the inside out. I was a practicing workaholic.

During these years I lived impatiently and impulsively. I was out of touch with myself. Because I was so busy, I had little time for reflection and contemplation, methods necessary to deeply understand oneself. I didn't know the meaning of quiet.

................................................................................

### STOP, LOOK, AND LISTEN
Allow yourself time to slow down and pay attention to your thoughts, ideas, and desires. Until you learn to listen to yourself, you'll have difficulty really listening to others.

................................................................................

It was during a difficult time in my life, at the height of my workaholism, that I had a rousing dream. I literally bolted out of bed and wrote it down, and it became a beacon for the path ahead.

The dream was as follows:

I was working in the woods, with sawdust under my fingernails from cutting firewood. I was wearing a red flannel shirt and jeans held up with broad, red suspenders. I was sweating from my labor, breathing heavily, when suddenly, in the midst of working, I noticed a salamander on the ground.

Then I awoke, crying.

I reached instantly for the journal I kept by my bed. I intuitively knew this dream contained an important message for me. I sat quietly in the predawn hours to consider each aspect of my dream.

While there are many who might interpret different aspects of the dream, I can only tell you what the dream meant, and did, for me.

I knew, instantly, that I had left an important part of my life behind—working in the woods and being close to nature. For me, cutting firewood had always been self-soothing, primitive, and basic. As old woodsmen say, I could warm myself three times with wood—cutting it, stacking it, and burning it. I had given up this hobby over time, as my vocation, extended schooling, and raising a family took more of my time. Busyness had taken its toll, and I needed to get my chainsaw out again.

What about getting sawdust under my fingernails? To me this again represented my desire to work with my hands, to do something "earthy." Sawdust also represented contact and identification with my heritage, as my grandparents and great-grandparents had emigrated from Sweden to build and work the lumber mills. I had walked the land where the mills used to be, dreaming of being a lumberman like them. As a young boy, I had watched my grandfather cut boards as he built houses. I needed to rediscover that aspect of my nature.

And what did the salamander represent? This is the element in my dream that brought tears. Some salamanders, you may know, can change colors in an effort to confuse their predators. To me, the salamander represented blending in and "changing my colors." I had lost my identity and unique distinction. I was "fitting in with the crowd," instead of doing what Thoreau recommended, following the music I hear.

Like all good dreams, this one stuck with me. It resonated with a deeper part of me for months, even years. The dream, which I came to believe was a message *from* my deepest self and *from* God *to* me, had a clear message that touched someplace deep inside: *It's time, David, to slow down. You're busy meeting everyone else's needs but few of your own. You need to get back to basics. You need to touch the earth and work with your hands; to see, smell, and touch something you have created. It's time to listen. Slow down, get some dirt and sawdust under your fingernails, and tune in to your true self. Move at your own natural pace, rather than some pace dictated for you.*

The dream did not, of course, give me a perfect road map back to myself. It simply awakened a longing for something different. The dream told me I was off course, changing too many colors, moving at someone else's pace. It was time to step back and reconsider my life direction and reconnect to a part of me I had lost.

## Ways to Listen to Yourself

Because I'd become familiar with moving fast, slowing down took some getting used to. After all, our society doesn't often promote taking time to know ourselves. Many people consider self-reflection an indulgence. But those who understand the way relationships work best understand that a connection to another person, particularly one's mate, comes out of a true connection with oneself.

Dag Hammarskjöld, former secretary-general of the United Nations, speaks eloquently on this point: "The more faithfully you listen to the voice within you, the better you will hear what is sounding outside. And only he who listens can speak. Is this the starting point of the road towards the union of your two dreams—to be allowed in clarity of mind to mirror life and in purity of heart to mold it?"[1]

Hammarskjöld is saying that it is critical to know your own voice, to recognize what you are feeling and thinking. It is in listening to yourself first that you learn to really listen to others. As we learn to give words to our own heartbeats, we more easily can help our mates give words to theirs.

There is only one way for our mates to know what makes our hearts skip a beat—we must tell them! There comes a time, and often many times, when we must be clear about what makes us excited, energized, passionate.

We can share with others only when we clearly understand ourselves. If we fail to take the time to listen to our own hearts, how can we share what is treasured within? We must take time to experience the treasure of our hearts, and as we do so, we can share it with our mates. Soul mates know what they feel, think, and want, and they have taken the time to nurture what is within.

### Listen within

Today dreaming is second nature to me. I can sit and daydream for hours, considering how to implement a new idea, how to make a million dollars, or what to call my next book—or two. Journaling helped me tune in to myself, so I could know what I thought and teach Christie how to nurture my dreams. I've journaled for many years, even practicing the art of daily journaling proposed by Julia Cameron in *The Artist's Way*. Cameron recommends a method of journaling called morning pages that I've found quite helpful. Quite simply, it is the practice of writing out three pages each morning. I write down anything that comes into my mind. I'm not attempting to produce great writing but to bring to the surface my concerns, desires, likes, dislikes, regrets, and plans.[2]

In addition to journaling, I make it a point to stop and listen to my feelings every now and then. As you begin to do this, it can be particularly helpful to reflect upon those times when you feel passion. What do you get excited about? What do you think about again and again? When do you feel intoxicated with possibility?

I believe in the value of knowing your dreams in order to sense and appreciate the direction of your life, but also as a means of sharing with your mate what is important to you. I like nothing more than to sit quietly with my wife and share new ideas and possibilities. I enjoy listening to others, encouraging them to dream big and often.

### Don't discount your emotions

Another way to become more aware of your own longings and passions is to embrace your emotions. Mark and Tricia were confused by their situation, but emotion became a bridge to one another. Emotion is also the beginning point for self-understanding.

Emotion is important; negative emotions often are a sign that something is amiss. Emotion is energy in motion, or if we've neglected

**DON'T DISCOUNT YOUR FEELINGS**
Emotion expressed is energy in motion;
emotion repressed stifles energy.

our feelings for too long, it is energy dammed up and stagnant. Emotion is precious, valuable, life directing.

Emotion is also one of the primary bridges we have to one another. Soul mates share emotions easily. The sadness I felt in my dream signaled an aching in my heart. My sadness wasn't just a small hurt, but rather grief from the loss of *me*. I had become someone else and missed myself terribly.

I was in therapy at the time and remember telling Dr. Hank, my psychologist, about the dream and what it meant to me. He didn't try to interpret the dream, understanding that only I could feel and sense what the dream meant.

I also shared the dream with my wife. She didn't try to interpret the dream either, but listened carefully, offering understanding and a sympathetic ear. Since the dream is nearly as powerful today as the day I had it, Christie and I can connect around it. I still must guard against losing touch with the earth, becoming too busy, and failing to listen to myself. Emotions, the kind that dreams often produce, help keep us grounded as well as tuned in to each other.

I must give my emotions room to be. Like coffee brewed in an old coffee pot, emotions need to percolate. As they percolate they tend to become clearer, deeper, and richer. Sitting with our feelings, we discover feelings beneath our feelings. Beneath our anger there is often hurt and sadness. Beneath our confusion we find ambivalence— mixed feelings about a particular person, place, or situation. There are layers to our feelings, just as there are layers to our relationships.

As we delve into our emotions, we learn more about ourselves. In fact, as we sit with our emotions, we find we know more than we thought we knew. We have more to share with our mates than we realized.

Mark and Tricia needed to spend time exploring who they had become and how they had drifted apart. As is often the case, they had not drifted too far apart that they needed to become friends again—it just took some extra effort. Mark still had many dormant qualities Tricia had found attractive in the beginning of their relationship, and Tricia unearthed qualities Mark desired as well.

### Be vulnerable

Sharing our dreams with our spouses requires something more: vulnerability. Mark's caution and tentative nature were understandable. He had been hurt as a child and then hurt again when rejected by Tricia. He was not eager to put himself in a position of being hurt again.

Tricia was cautious as well, though she was more willing to readily share her needs with Mark. Outspoken, she was more in touch with her vulnerable self, ready to make their marriage work.

Sharing dreams is not necessarily easy work. You can imagine my anxiety about sharing my dream with my wife, not to mention my psychologist. What would they think? When we reveal our dreams, we allow others to see us without defense. "This is your naked self," my dream announced. "This is what you really think, beneath your conscious thinking." To share it with someone required safety, empathy, and protection—all ingredients we discussed in the last chapter.

Both Tricia and Mark were determined to provide safety to each other. They recognized the fragility of their relationship and the importance of providing protection from criticism. Slowly Mark began to open up to Tricia. He began to teach her how to nurture his dreams. In one of our early sessions, he talked about one of his desires.

"I don't want to work so much. I'm ready to slow down and work on our marriage. I really do want a best friend again. I feel lonely in my apartment. I miss our times of sitting together, listening to Linda Ronstadt and sharing our day. I know you need more from me, and I need more from you. I need you to be interested in my day. I need you to take interest in my love of travel, music, and books. I want to read together, so we can talk about the characters the way we used to."

Tricia was quiet, caught in rapt attention as Mark spoke.

"You haven't talked to me like this in five years," she said softly. "Of course I'd love to do those things. I'm willing to do those things."

"I haven't really known you cared about what was important to me," Mark said.

"Ouch!" Tricia responded.

"I didn't say it to hurt you, Tricia," Mark said, "but I think we both have something to learn about letting the other know that we care what they think. I want to know that you care what I think."

"I'd like the same," Tricia said defensively.

"So you both want the same thing. That gives us a great starting place," I said enthusiastically. "Let's talk about how couples get there."

Tricia and Mark were learning how to be vulnerable with each other. They began practicing letting one another know they valued what the other thought, building a stronger relationship in the process. It was exciting for me to watch them become best friends again.

## Best Friends

Do you think about being best friends with your mate? Have you considered that soul mates are, above all, best friends?

Ed Wheat, author of *Love Life for Every Married Couple*, offers profound instruction when it comes to being soul-mate friends with your mate. Wheat reminds us that the basis of soul-mate friendship is *phileo* love.

But what is phileo love? Phileo love is illustrated by Jonathan and David's relationship. "Jonathan became one in spirit with David, and he loved him as himself" (1 Samuel 18:1). These men were far more than friends—they were emotional brothers.

God also loves with a phileo love: "The Father dearly loves the Son and discloses to (shows) Him everything that He Himself does" (John 5:20, AMP).

Wheat goes on to describe how phileo love is our basis for soul-mate love. "The fond friendship of *phileo* takes on added intensity and enjoyment as part of the multi-faceted love bond of husband and wife. When two people in marriage share themselves—their lives, their dreams, and all they are—they develop this love of mutual affection, rapport, and comradeship. They care for each other tenderly. They hold each other dear. This is cherishing!"[3]

Teaching your mate to nurture your dreams comes from a basis of friendship. Do you take time to nurture phileo love with your mate? Here are a few ideas to foster friendship as well as teach your mate to nurture your dreams:

*Let your mate know what is important to you.* Remember, your mate cannot read your mind. Let him or her know what you need and want. Talk about your dreams, hopes, and desires.

*Let your mate know what traits you'd like appreciation for.* While this may feel awkward, ask your mate to notice specific traits. If you want to be recognized for helping out around the house, ask for it. If you want recognition for the efforts you put in with your children's education, make that clear. Ask for appreciation. Let your spouse know that you appreciate when he or she offers you encouragement.

*Ask for more.* Yes, you read correctly. Ask for more. Be vulnerable and ask for what you need. When you voice your request in a tone of caring and concern, it is more likely to be met with receptivity.

*Tell your mate you are interested in what he or she needs as well.* Genuine interest has been called the height of love. Show your interest in what interests your mate, and ask for the same in return.

*Share.* There are no shortcuts to friendship—you must share. You must share what you think, feel, and want. You must share your dreams, fears, hopes, and opinions. Though difficult at times, and frightening at other times, you must share. The moment you notice yourself holding back, reflect on what is going on. Is this a time to hold back out of wisdom, or are you beginning to build a wall between you and your mate?

Each of these tasks helps knit you closer to your mate. Take time to practice each of them, again and again. As you honor your mate's feelings and thoughts with your complete attention, he or she will share more. As you make it clear that you value your mate's dreams, he or she will dream more with you.

## Making Requests

Teaching your mate to nurture your dreams is comprised largely of making requests—something not easy for most of us to do. Raised with rugged individualism and often required to fend for ourselves as children, many of us don't know the first thing about asking for our needs to be met. We are beginners when it comes to teaching our mates how we want to be treated.

If you are like me, you've also been hurt a time or two. When someone hurts us, it's only natural to pull away.

"I can make it on my own," we say. "I can treat myself better than anyone else can treat me."

But is that really true? It certainly sounds good on the surface. However, I wonder about its authenticity.

Recently I talked to the delightful owner of a retail shop on Cape Cod, Massachusetts. I told her I was writing a book about soul mates.

"Oh, I don't need anyone else to be my soul mate," she said enthusiastically. "I'm my own soul mate."

She smiled and waited for my response. I wasn't sure what to say, partly since her statement smacked against the premise of my book—that we can be soul mates with another person.

The shop owner, who appeared to be in her late fifties, said she was happily single. "No one can treat me as well as I can treat myself. I am my own best friend."

I drove away less than convinced. While I certainly want to be a good friend to myself, I want my wife to be my best friend more. While I want to treat myself well, I rather enjoy it when my wife dotes on me, makes a fuss over me, and cheers me on. The owner's words didn't ring true for me. Christie really can treat me better than I can treat myself, and we become soul mates in the process.

Could it be that the shop owner and people like her have been hurt and decided not to risk getting close? Have they learned that there will always be disappointment if they hope for someone to meet their needs? Possibly so.

There is a huge risk in making the move from mate to soul mate, and that risk involves asking for what we need. There is no way your mate can read your mind. Even the best listeners aren't going to get it right without your clarification.

So what have I taught Christie about myself and my dreams? Here are a few things:

Like her, I love the ocean.
I want to be in the water, on the water, or near the water.
I love quiet evenings, snuggling on the couch with her.
I love children.
I love thinking of new book ideas, speaking topics, and ways to encourage others.
I want to spend more time writing, reading, sailing, and walking the beach.

While I could do all of these things on my own, each one is enhanced with my soul mate. But for any of them to occur with my soul mate, I must risk asking for something. What might that look like?

I ask Christie if she will take a drive to the ocean with me.
I ask Christie if she will go with me for a walk on the beach.
I ask Christie to spend a quiet evening with me, perhaps with
   a fire and a good book, snuggling on our couch.
I ask Christie if she will go with me to see our grandson.
I ask Christie if she will sit with me to discuss new book ideas.
I ask Christie if she will take a trip with me where I can write,
   we can read, and we can walk beaches together.

Now, take a look at my list again. Consider my requests. What do you think the chances are of Christie turning down any of those requests, especially if asked with a warm and generous heart? I assure you she will gladly meet each and every one of those requests, leading to a closer and warmer relationship.

I hope the pieces are beginning to come together for you. This eighth task—teaching your mate to nurture your dreams—combined with nurturing your mate's dreams, has the possibility of creating a powerful connection. This vibrant, dynamic connection is one experienced by far too few people, but available to all.

What is it about dream sharing that unites our hearts to our mates? I think it is the depth at which we share. When I talk to my mate about those things that stir her heart most wildly, creating a soft, safe place for her to dream, and she does the same for me, we touch each other more deeply than at any other time. This is the profound difference between being mates and being soul mates.

Soul mates can often finish each other's sentences. Why? Because they know what each other thinks. Soul mates anticipate each other's needs. Why? Because they have spent intimate time together and know what is important to one another. Soul mates have peeled off the layers of protection, chosen vulnerability, and then encouraged their mates to dream larger than they thought possible. Remember, when we encourage our mates to dream, we become larger in the process.

## Weekly Quiz

Before you can teach your mate to nurture your dreams, you must recognize those dreams within yourself. How are you doing at recognizing and honoring your own dreams? Many people struggle in giving themselves permission to dream. Not surprisingly, they really have difficulty asking their mates to nurture their dreams as well. Yet sharing and nurturing each other's dreams is a powerful way to connect to each other.

How might you handle the following scenario:

You have had a secret desire to work with children professionally, perhaps as a teacher. You are uncertain as to whether this desire has any possibility, since you've never worked in this area before. You

a) keep this dream to yourself, fearing sounding foolish or fearing your mate might criticize your dream.

b) share your ideas with your mate, confident that he or she will either give you honest, caring feedback or be encouraging with you.

........................................................................................

## PUTTING IT INTO PRACTICE THIS WEEK

1. If you don't think you can put your dreams into words, consider trying the journal technique on page 131. You don't have to use it every day; however, you might be surprised to find that this technique helps you express your dreams and hopes for the future.

2. Share a dream you had while sleeping that still comes to mind often. What does it tell you about your dreams or fears?

3. Listening and encouraging your spouse's dream is sometimes easier than sharing your own. If that is the case for you or your spouse, discuss the reasons behind the reluctance. In what ways can you better support one another's hopes and dreams?

*Week 9*

# PREPARING YOUR BEST TO MEET YOUR SPOUSE'S BEST

*To change how we see things takes falling in love.*
*Then the same becomes altogether different.*
—James Hillman, *The Soul's Code*

**SIGNS THAT YOUR BEST NEEDS TO MEET YOUR SPOUSE'S BEST**
1. You view home more as a freeway rest stop than a four-star hotel.
2. Your conversations with your spouse are as meaningful and deep as your exchange with the unseen attendant at your local drive-through.
3. *Civility? Does that have something to do with the War between the States?*
4. Your spouse has a lot of amazing qualities—but how come they only come out when other people are around?
5. You still cannot believe your spouse told that embarrassing story about you at the last company party.

While I love to read books on the craft of writing, like *The Artist's Way* by Julia Cameron, *On Writing* by Stephen King, and *Bird by Bird* by Anne Lamott, recently I have also developed an appreciation for books on interior design, especially those on creating a welcoming home and nurturing friendships.

This inclination was unexpected, since I have no ability in interior design. In fact, I'm color-blind and have little sense of balance, layout, or design in the home. I have no appreciation for textures, lighting, or any of the other particulars associated with decorating and entertaining.

I can, however, sense when a home offers warmth, character, and caring. I know when a house feels like a home and can tell when visitors feel like valued guests. I know when people feel invited, welcomed, and appreciated after spending an evening with us.

Perhaps this interest in home interiors and environments evolved from my work with the interiors of persons, my care for their souls. Maybe I'm more attuned to people and their natural surroundings since I spend every workday helping people make peace with their worlds. I want people to feel comfortable around me as I work with them, and now, with my interest in interiors, I'm also interested in how they experience their personal spaces.

Interior designer and author Alexandra Stoddard first alerted me to the small, personal touches we can add to our homes to help our family, friends, and guests feel at home. Stoddard gave me new ideas on how to make a house a home, ways to bring life into a house, and how to treat special friends. Though when she began her writing career Stoddard wrote exclusively about home interiors, much of her writing today focuses on the interiors of personal relationships and ways to enhance and enliven interpersonal relationships. She espouses living happily every day, and she believes healthy relationships improve our quality of life.

From reading her books, I get the sense that every day is a treat in the Stoddard home and that everyone is treated as a guest. I can't picture anyone there rushing around, eating chips out of the bag, or slurping coffee as he or she rushes out the door. Stoddard models another way to live—a more genteel way than most of us are accustomed to.

Stoddard's writing has influenced me greatly, particularly as I've thought about our ninth task: preparing your best to meet your spouse's best. When my best meets Christie's best, good things are going to happen. When I'm the best person I can be, fully tuned in to my dreams, passions, and feelings, and I encourage my wife to be her best, embracing her dreams, passions, and feelings, we connect in a powerful way.

Being our best with each other means living beyond our mundane routines. What would you do if you were invited to have tea with the queen of England? Wouldn't you dust off your book on etiquette, dress up, and then go, prepared for a lively and dignified afternoon?

Like Alexandra Stoddard, Christie is an interior designer with similar gifts of hospitality, style, and elegance.

Perhaps I'm the latecomer to the party, but until I met Christie, I didn't know what interior designers did. I assumed they just helped clients pick out curtains for the bedroom and wallpaper for the living room. Little did I know that excellent designers do more listening than just about anything else so they can bring out the best in people and their homes.

I like to watch Christie in action, whether she is designing a home or entertaining. I watch her enable people to create welcoming rooms rather than simply throwing together some functional items. I watch her make the simplest gathering an event as she makes color, texture, taste, and sound come together in a pleasing way. Because she also has a lively and engaging personality, every setting is a party that would make Stoddard proud.

Recently we had our grown children home for breakfast. We had crepes. However, we didn't simply have crepes. Are you kidding? We had strawberries, blueberries, raspberries, syrups, and sugars, along with sausages and orange juice. As if this were not enough, the table settings were decorated in a beach theme. We all sat down together for a festive breakfast.

As everyone gathered for our meal, we all knew we were to be on our best behavior. This wasn't a "grab something and go" event. This was like tea with the queen in midafternoon. This was Cinderella's ball. This was breakfast at Tiffany's. We all knew there was a protocol to follow, all inspired by Christie.

Some of you might be thinking, *I'd rather grab a bowl of Wheaties and be off.* While that may be your preference today, I want to entice you with crepes and orange juice. You have an opportunity, with every meal, every greeting, and every interaction, to bring out the best in both you and your spouse. This week centers on learning to bring out the best in each other—starting when you sit down to breakfast.

## Civility

*But real people don't live that way! Who in the world would slow down long enough to have a seven-course breakfast?*

How right you are. When real people get up in the morning, they generally scurry to the bathroom, grumble about too little sleep, and fly out the door feeling as if they have too much to do. Often living beyond their means, couples are stressed out and treat each other like the crotchety neighbor they never liked, not their soul mate.

Stoddard's writing is not especially exciting. She is not overly eloquent and doesn't say anything earth shattering. She doesn't shock, awe, or enrage—but she does inspire me as she advocates bringing civility back into our lives.

........................................................................................

### BE CIVIL-IZED
Our society doesn't do much to encourage it, but taking the time to extend courtesy and respect to other family members generally encourages them to treat you in the same way.

........................................................................................

Civility. There's a word you may not have used in a while. What do I mean by the word *civility*? I mean being polite to others, being courteous, caring about others. I mean bringing back a touch of formality, distinction, and class to our lives. I mean expressing an interest in others.

In his book *The Civility Solution*, P. M. Forni tells us we need to confront the lack of civility in an assertive but nonaggressive way. Failing to do so, he says, will ensure that destructive behavior continues. We teach people how to treat us. We let them know, directly and indirectly, what they can get away with when interacting with us.[1]

But what does civility look like in relationships? How might we cultivate it as we strive to bring out the best in our mates?

Forni suggests that when we act civilly, others will act that way too. When we expect others to treat us well, they often do. When we confront others on their aggressive behavior and tell them how we wish to be treated, they're often willing to do so. When met with an offense, he suggests we state the facts, inform the other person of the impact he or she has had upon us, and request that the hurtful behavior not be repeated.

Last year my wife and I attended my son's medical school graduation. The day before his graduation ceremonies at Carnegie Hall in Manhattan, the university hosted a formal garden party on campus.

Hors d'oeuvres and beverages were served in party tents. Attire for the event was casual formal, with men wearing collared shirts and sport coats and women wearing pantsuits or summer dresses. Everyone knew exactly how to dress and behave—and they did!

A bit unfamiliar with such formality, I watched others for cues on how to behave. I watched how others carried themselves, their drinks, and their dishes; how they engaged others in conversation; and what small courtesies the guests extended to one another.

Was this event a bit stuffy? Perhaps, but my, was it fun! We were all looking our best, acting our best, treating others with respect. It was a lesson in how to behave with others.

I left that garden party wondering what would happen if we brought a bit of formality and civility into our marriages. I decided we'd be a lot better off.

## Behaving, All the Time

When spouses are both at their best, their relationship is characterized by elegance and courtesy. Spouses who are willing to be on their best behavior all the time know good behavior improves relationships.

This concept isn't rocket science. I am living proof that when I walk through the door at night and act grouchy, touchy, and perhaps even a bit mean-spirited, things will go badly. I really have tried it both ways: being a nice guy, sensitive to Christie's needs, and chivalrous; and acting self-centered, insensitive, and even unkind. I doubt I need to tell you the results.

When the best David shows up, he is rewarded handsomely with kindness, sensitivity, and warmth. These are all qualities I greatly appreciate. I love it when Christie thanks me for being the best David I can be. I love being rewarded for positive behavior.

However, there are two questions we must address.

One, isn't it a lot of work to behave nicely all the time? Yes. Being on your best behavior requires attention, concentration, and refinement of skills you already have. But you must keep this behavior in the forefront of your mind. It won't come naturally until you've made a habit of it.

Many Americans were riveted to their televisions during the 2008 Olympics, anxious to see if Michael Phelps would surpass the unprecedented number of medals collected by Mark Spitz. Phelps appeared up for the competition, and we saw him in his glory, taking on and beating the competition as if they weren't even competitors. Phelps took his natural talent and then practiced—and practiced—leading to victory. Ready for the challenge, he made the rigors of competition look easy.

When interviewed, Phelps explained that he'd been practicing four to eight hours a day for four years. One of the questions he was asked repeatedly was, "Isn't it difficult to practice all the time?" He admitted that the practice regimen to become the best was grueling. He hadn't expected it to be easy but kept reminding himself of the prize at the end. He dedicated himself to becoming the best swimmer in history, through years of rigorous discipline.

While "behaving nicely" isn't an Olympic sport, at least not yet, I wonder how many of us would dedicate ourselves to being the best husband or wife in history? Is it worth aiming for the gold medal? Do we even care if we're seen and appreciated for being an incredible husband or wife?

Yes, it is a lot of work to behave nicely all the time. Yes, it is an incredible amount of work. But it is worth it. Of course, you won't get an actual gold medal—just a soul mate who adores you. Not bad if you ask me.

The second question you may be asking yourself is, *Why do I have to behave nicely all the time? Aren't there shortcuts?* Why is it so critical to consistently behave with dignity, chivalry, and perhaps even a little bit of style and panache? Because being your best demands concentration, attention, and perfect practice. Behaving nicely two days out of four is not the mark of a soul mate and will not win the heart of a soul mate.

For you to *be* a soul mate, and for you to be *with* your soul mate, you must be your best consistently. Being your best must be on the frontal lobe of your brain—that part of our anatomy that reminds us of the important tasks of the day. As we remind ourselves why we are doing what we're doing, we'll maintain motivation to keep doing it. You must have laser-like focus on being the best person you can be, dedicated to being respectful, loving, kind, and generous. These are the characteristics of a soul mate and are sure to win the heart—your prize—of your soul mate.

## Breakdown in Civility

A young couple who had been experiencing a great deal of conflict came to see me recently. Darcy was dressed casually in jeans and a blouse, chatting enthusiastically with Ken when I came into the waiting room. Ken, a heavyset man dressed in jeans and a sweatshirt, rose and approached me with a gregarious attitude, almost overly friendly.

As they sat down in my office, I asked them what had brought them to counseling. Both twenty-three years old and married for only a year, Ken and Darcy were already in trouble.

"We have the bad habit of saying what we think," Ken said, smiling. "She gets her feelings hurt easily, and when I tell her not to have her feelings hurt, she just gets angrier. I don't really say things to hurt her. . . ."

Darcy rolled her eyes at Ken's comment.

"What do you think, Darcy?" I asked.

"That's not exactly the way I see it," Darcy said, looking sternly at Ken. "We both say things to hurt each other when we're upset. Sometimes even when we're not upset. We can snip at each other over the smallest things. It's hurting our marriage."

"Yeah," Ken replied. "That's just the way I was raised. We said what was on our mind. I know that's no excuse. I need to find out why I blurt hurtful things out. Darcy is the last person I want to hurt."

"I *do* get my feelings hurt, whether I should or not," said Darcy. "Then I push away. I really don't want to distance myself from Ken, but I don't want him talking harshly to me. He's not the only one who speaks what's on his mind though," she said, coming to Ken's defense. "I can be pretty blunt myself."

"She can have a sharp tongue," Ken said. "I don't much like it when she bites at me either. This is just not the way we want to be with each other."

"So I'm curious," I said, "if neither of you likes the other being blunt, why do you continue doing it?"

Ken looked at Darcy and smiled.

"Don't get us wrong," Ken said. "It's not like we're always that way. When things are good, they're very good."

Darcy jumped in. "And when they're bad, they're pretty bad. We really love each other. We're nice to each other most of the time. But we can slip into pretty ugly words quickly."

"Yes," I said. "But you didn't really answer me, you guys. How come you continue talking to each other in ways you know are destructive and hurtful?"

"Well," Darcy said sheepishly, "we thought maybe you could shed some light on that. We know we're tearing each other up, even though we love each other. It doesn't make any sense. We just keep doing it, especially if we're angry. Then we do it even more."

"Let's take a history and see if we find any clues there," I suggested. "Ken, let's start with you."

Ken explained that he had been raised in a middle-class home in the country. His father was a log-truck driver, and his mother worked as a paraprofessional in the local school district. He has three brothers. His father had an alcohol problem, and there was occasional violence between his parents. The language between everyone in his family was colorful and lively.

"Nobody cared much if they hurt someone's feelings," Ken said brashly. "You were expected to get over it. We were loud but loving. There were a lot of good times, and a few bad times."

"Can you see anything about the way you were raised that might explain why you talk to Darcy the way you do?"

### UNINTENTIONAL NEGLECT
Many couples never saw their own parents model courtesy toward one another; as a result, they tend to be casual and careless in their own interactions with their spouses.

"I can!" Darcy said quickly. "When we're at their house, it's chaos. Everybody's talking and nobody's listening. Feelings are hurt all the time, though nobody talks about it."

Ken shrugged.

"You don't agree?" I asked, looking to Ken.

"We speak our mind," he said. "Like I said before, we say it the way it is. That's all there is to it."

"And feelings get hurt," Darcy said. "You can't tell me your mom doesn't get her feelings hurt by your dad."

"Yes, she sure does," Ken said reluctantly.

"And how about your family?" I asked, looking at Darcy.

"Wow! Me," she began. "Our home wasn't any *Little House on the Prairie*, that's for sure. My dad left when I was eight, and I was raised by my grandparents and sometimes my mom. Me and my brother were left to fend for ourselves most of the time. I was living on the streets by the time I was seventeen. If it hadn't been for meeting Ken, who knows where I'd be."

"So you didn't learn much about how to treat another person," I said.

"We didn't learn how to be kind and loving, especially when there is conflict," Darcy added. "This is all new to me."

"A lot of people just say what's on their minds," I said, "but it really goes against scriptural teaching about speaking the truth in love and treating each other with honor and dignity. And you can see the results of saying whatever you feel."

Darcy and Ken were ready for a change. They needed to learn how to speak in ways that were respectful. It didn't come naturally, however.

Let's zero in on some of the factors that contributed to Darcy and Ken's problems and that kept them (like many other couples) from becoming soul mates. As we review these traits, consider which of them may be at work in your marriage.

*Casual attitudes.* Ken and Darcy were definitely products of their upbringing. It wasn't so much that they were neglected as children; they simply were never taught the fine art of speaking clearly *and* lovingly.

In Ephesians 4:15 (NLT), the apostle Paul urges us to "speak the truth in love," suggesting it's possible to say *everything* in a way that will elevate a conversation, rather than bring it down. There is a way to approach another person, on any topic, that conveys the following:

- I will respect you.
- I will not be condescending or derogatory.

- I will treat you with dignity.
- I will be clear with you about what I feel, think, and want.
- I will not call you names, tell you what to think, or cause unnecessary division between us.

Ken and Darcy weren't playing by these rules. In fact, they really didn't have any rules. They were not focused and intentional about treating each other with respect. Their casual attitude was harming their relationship. Once they realized the toll this approach was taking on their new marriage, they resolved to change.

*Unintentional living.* It's not really surprising that Ken and Darcy had such a casual attitude toward their communication style. Like many couples, they were living unintentionally—meaning they moved from moment to moment, unaware of the connection between them. They didn't think through the consequences of their actions, and they certainly didn't plan ahead. They had no vision for how they wanted their relationship to be or to become, and subsequently, they meandered haphazardly. Only when their relationship began to deteriorate did they learn firsthand the damage that living this way can cause.

In my book *Are You Really Ready for Love?* I espouse the importance of living intentionally. I talk about the importance of having a road map, not only for your life, but for your love life.

Where do you want your relationship to go? In what direction are you currently moving? Do you need to steer the relationship in a new direction?

These questions will help you live intentionally. They will help you slow down, stop if necessary, and recalibrate your course. Ken and Darcy definitely needed to reconsider the direction of their marriage. If they continued living impulsively, shooting from the hip and saying whatever came to mind, they would continue hurting each other.

*Loss of trust.* When you're uncertain what your mate is going to say or when he or she is going to blow up at you, there will be little trust between you. If you're not certain you'll always be treated with dignity, your trust for your mate will suffer. If you're not absolutely convinced your mate will always act with love, you're going to be on your guard. Soul-mate love cannot thrive in this atmosphere of uncertainty, disrespect, or lack of trust.

Thomas Moore, author of *Soul Mates*, speaks to this issue. He talks about the challenges inherent in relationships where there are messy moments of betrayal, loss of trust, and subsequent questions about respect. He says, "It isn't easy to expose your soul to another, to risk such vulnerability, hoping that the other person will be able to tolerate your own irrationality. It may also be difficult, no matter how open-minded you are, to be receptive as another reveals her soul to you."

Moore then offers us hope: "Within an individual, too, intimacy calls for love and acceptance of the soul's less rational outposts. . . . Honoring that aspect of the soul that is irrational and extreme, we have far fewer expectations of perfection, in ourselves and in others."[2]

*Loss of respect.* Moore's premise that a bit of messiness is inevitable must be accepted with caution—we cannot presume upon our mates' patience and understanding, telling them, as Ken told Darcy, not to take our cutting remarks personally. This argument might fly once, perhaps even twice, but at some point it will lead to a profound loss of respect.

Slowly, insidiously, walls will be erected. At some level spouses decide they won't expose themselves to further hurt. They create distance—palpable distance.

*Loss of dignity.* With every angry outburst or sharp word spoken, we undercut our mates' dignity. A biting remark here, a sarcastic comment there—all demonstrate a lack of respect.

This, of course, goes completely against the Scriptures and against what I believe most of us truly value. Most of us, if pressed, would agree that we have been created in and for dignity. Even though sarcasm and cutting comments had become commonplace in Ken and Darcy's relationship, deep inside they realized they were damaging one another's dignity—whether or not they could have put that into words.

Even when others hurt us, most of us would say we don't have the right to hurt them in return. Even when we experience betrayal, most people won't stoop to a similar level of faithlessness, as much as we might be tempted to do so. Revenge may be in our thoughts, but it's probably not in our ideal repertoire.

Recently I read the love story of Elizabeth Barrett Browning. Raised in a well-to-do nineteenth-century family in rural England, she was part of a loving family. When she was fifteen, however, she fell ill. Life became more difficult when her mother died, leaving behind twelve children. Elizabeth's father would not give any of his children permission to marry. Elizabeth apparently gave in to her illness and spent most of her time in bed, determined never to love a man.

That all changed, however, when she was thirty-nine. Susan Baur shares her version of the love story in *The Love of Your Life*: "Then into her darkened sickroom walked the thirty-three-year-old poet Robert Browning, prepared to worship both her and her work." Though he'd admired her writing from afar, once he met her and their relationship deepened, Browning fell in love with the dark-haired, petite Elizabeth. Before long, he was talking marriage, suggesting they could then go to Italy and write poetry together.

As we can imagine, this was a very tantalizing offer. Barrett's father, however, was not as excited about the idea. Barrett's father adamantly opposed the friendship.

Yet Browning had an increasingly powerful effect on Barrett. While initially reluctant to follow her heart, and go against her father's wishes, "gradually, the invalid poet began seeing herself more as Browning saw her and less as her father saw her."[3]

It is wonderful to see the change that comes over her. Barrett out of love is a very different person from Barrett in love. Once she was treated with dignity and respect, Elizabeth Barrett grew stronger, healthier, and courageous. She went on to marry Browning. "The love of a lifetime initiates such sweeping changes," Baur writes, "that it inevitably breaks former ties in ways that are unexpected and painful."[4]

The Brownings enjoyed a mutually nurturing marriage until Elizabeth's death fifteen years later. "I love thee with the breath, smiles, tears of all my life!" she had written. "And, if God choose, I shall but love thee better after death."[5]

The Brownings offer inspiration to the rest of us—can we bring some of this majesty and dignity to our marriages? Will you add dignity to your marriage?

*Settling for the status quo.* The Brownings seem to have had a loftier vision for marriage than many of us have today. With their sights set high, they expected to give much to their relationship, and consequently they knew they would receive much in return. In contrast, Ken and Darcy entered marriage without considering how they could build a healthier relationship than had been modeled by their parents.

It has been said that we expect too much from our marriages. Giving that some thought, I heartily disagree. I think that, in large part,

---

**DON'T SETTLE FOR THE STATUS QUO**
Our fast-paced, impersonal world does little to recognize people's worth. However, home should be the place where the dignity of each family member is affirmed and celebrated.

---

we expect too little. We are often willing to allow our marriages to drift. We are prone to shoot low rather than to aim high.

What if we had to endure more to attain our loved one? What if we had to wait, conquer, struggle to win the hand of our beloved? Would our marriages then contain the magical quality we wonder about, the love of a soul mate?

*Selfishness.* Love "is not rude," the apostle Paul wrote to the church at Corinth in what is called the Bible's love chapter. It "is not self-seeking, it is not easily angered, it keeps no record of wrongs" (1 Corinthians 13:5).

These words have always made me pause. If love is not rude and I am rude, what does that say about me? If love is not self-seeking and I *do* seek my own way, what does that say about me?

The words of Paul are piercing because they challenge us to move outside our natural inclinations and into the world of love—which is a different world. This new world, where we are transformed by God's love and the love of our mates, is a world where we are no longer selfish. We truly want the best for our spouses. And we want to give them *our* best. In fact, if we don't want to give our best to our mates, we must ask ourselves whether we truly love them.

The apostle John builds upon Paul's teaching: "But if we walk in the light, as he is in the light, we have fellowship with one another, and the blood of Jesus, his Son, purifies us from all sin" (1 John 1:7). If we are filled with God's love, we will be changed. We will no longer attempt to will ourselves to love our mates but will love them because we are loved by God. Our love, in one sense, is an act of obedience because it's done whether we feel like it or not. Neither Ken nor Darcy had ever witnessed this form of self-sacrifice in their homes while growing up. No wonder they fell into old patterns as they set up their own household.

Soul mates tune in to their mates, seeking ways to love them, encourage their dreams, and give dignity to their lives. This love isn't painful and unmanageable, but it enhances the giver as much as the recipient.

*Busyness.* Giving the best to one another means we must make room for love, allowing other activities to take a lower priority. This, however, often goes against what might feel natural. After all, so many things in our lives clamor for attention. We rush around in a state of busyness, multitasking, tending to this and that, while love is placed on the back burner. How can we possibly give our best to anything—from our vocation to matters of the heart—if we don't treat it as important? I am so glad Ken and Darcy came to see me early in their marriage, before the pressures of career and children made it even more difficult for them to make time for one another.

Matters of the heart need tending. Relationships need constant nurturing, not haphazard attention. Busyness and tending to your soul mate do not coexist easily.

Too many times in my marriage I've tried to fit my relationship into the leftover "nooks and crannies" of my life—and my marriage reflected that. When I give leftovers to my wife, she senses it. When she gives leftovers to me, I don't like it either.

Have you made room in your relationship for love to flourish? Are there other things, activities or even compulsive behaviors that need to be pruned to make room for love?

## Restoring Style

Style. Now there's a word I'll bet you've not heard associated with marriage. Style—the stuff that made legends out of actors and actresses of yesteryear—such as Cary Grant, Lauren Bacall, Frank Sinatra, Peter Lawford, and Grace Kelly. These people evoked images of class, of style.

While I'm in no way suggesting that each of these people had the character to back his or her screen image, there is still something to be learned from their portrayals of lovely, caring, and sensitive individuals on-screen. Such style and dignity is evident in the marriages of soul mates.

What do I mean by style?

- Style carries with it a hint of formality, without being stiff.
- Style carries with it a touch of the suave and debonair, without being standoffish.
- Style carries with it the presence of respect, without the suggestion of presumption.
- Style carries with it the presence of distinction, without being distant.
- Style carries with it a hint of flirtation, playfulness, and lightheartedness, without being risqué.

When I think of style in marriage, I fondly remember the relationship of Jack and Evelyn Boyd. Jack passed away several years ago after working in the grocery business for fifty years. Evelyn retired from a

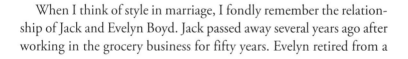

**CLASS ACT**
Never underestimate the power of two spouses being courteous and classy in their interactions. Not only will you benefit, other people will stop and take notice.

long career in nursing. Each always had a ready smile, a gentle touch, and an unsolicited act of kindness for the other.

Having met the Boyds through professional circles, our family became fast friends with this couple. (In fact, our two sons considered them their adopted grandparents.) While distinctly middle-class, Jack and Evelyn lived like royalty. They treated each other with profound respect, always exhibiting politeness and dignity. I remember many evenings at their home where they made every meal an event. Evelyn loved to put ceramic nameplates in front of the dinnerware when she had guests over for one of Jack's seven-course gourmet meals. With just a hint of formality, they made our family and other guests feel special.

What if we were to reintroduce a hint of these characteristics to our marriages? What if we decided to stop taking our mates for granted, and instead added a bit of panache? Would you like to be treated like a prince or princess? I certainly would—and am!

## Our Best, Together

When your best meets your spouse's best, something powerful called *potentiation* occurs. Medical professionals and pharmaceutical companies often use this term to describe the action that occurs when one drug combines with another to create something more powerful than either alone. Likewise, the benefits to your marriage can exponentially exceed the efforts of two spouses devoted to giving one another their best.

The combination of your best traits with your spouse's best traits creates something more powerful and exciting than what either of you brings to the table individually. This truth is universal and timeless, and we shouldn't be surprised about this possibility in marriage. God originally said man should not be alone and created a helpmate for him. Man and woman, together, reflect the image of God.

Potentiation is a powerful concept. Picture two rivers coming together. There is generally a bit of turbulence where they meet, but ultimately they create a more powerful force than either river alone. The same occurs when your best meets the best of your mate.

Consider once more the marriage of Robert and Elizabeth Barrett Browning. While both people were fine poets in their own right, critics credit their marriage as the force that brought out the best in each of them. They adored one another, and out of that affection flowed mutual encouragement and gentle criticism of their writing. In addition, the move to Italy opened new worlds to Elizabeth, greatly expanding the material from which she had to work. For his part, Robert, a relatively unknown poet at the time of his marriage, became one of the most respected Victorian poets. After his death in 1889, he was even honored by being buried in the Poet's Corner of Westminster Abbey.

You and your spouse may or may not share a love of poetry, but that doesn't mean you can't experience potentiation. You can set selfishness aside, leave immaturity and presumption outside the relationship, and choose to be the best mate you can be. If you choose to bring your best to the relationship, you will encourage your mate to do the same. Together, you will be a formidable combination.

## Weekly Quiz

What better place to show off our best than in our marriages? No one deserves our best more than our mates. Marriage is where we should show off our best behavior, though this isn't always easy to do.

Consider how you might handle the following situation:

You're meeting another couple for dinner. When your wife comes down the stairs ready to leave, you

a) tell her she took so long getting ready that you're going to be late; without waiting for her response, you walk ahead of her out the door.

b) reach for her hand and tell her how lovely she looks and how excited you are to spend the evening with her.

## PUTTING IT INTO PRACTICE THIS WEEK

1. If your family is like most, dinner is often a rushed affair. Pick a night this week with little on the schedule when your family can eat together slowly, enjoying unhurried discussion and following

your best manners. If you have kids, don't expect them to suddenly have impeccable table manners, but do politely point out the ways good manners can make mealtime more pleasant for everyone. Afterward, talk about the experience with one another. How did it feel to be less rushed, have time to listen, and be courteous to one another?

2. Consider watching a movie like *Sense & Sensibility* or *Kate & Leopold*, in which the main characters are generally courteous and well-mannered toward one another. What did you take away from the film that you might apply to your own relationship?

3. Does your family put a premium on civility and courtesy? If not, why not? Talk with your spouse about how family life might look different if you did.

4. Can you think of a couple like the Boyds (see pages 153–154) who display elegance, style, and class in their interactions with each other? If you were to emulate one of their behaviors, which would it be?

# UNLEASHING THE POWER OF POSITIVE GOSSIPING

*Practice mindful speech by using Socrates' triple filter.*
*Ask yourself: Is it true? Is it kind? Is it helpful?*
—Lucy MacDonald

## SIGNS THAT YOU NEED TO DISCOVER THE POWER OF POSITIVE GOSSIPING

1. You're afraid that if you say something nice about your spouse, he or she will get a big head.
2. Your idea of a compliment is telling your spouse, "Thanks for finally painting the front door. When are you going to get around to caulking the windows?"
3. You'd never gossip about your spouse—after all, your mom always told you, "If you can't say something nice about someone, don't say anything at all."
4. You'll be more than happy to give your spouse a compliment. Just as soon as he or she does something to deserve it.
5. You've complained about your spouse so much and for so long that you're close to setting a new world record (the Guinness people are coming on Tuesday).

"Sticks and stones may break my bones, but words will never hurt me." I learned early in life how misguided this statement really is.

I grew up in a family of five kids, and words were flying among us all the time. Sometimes they were nice, friendly words—often they were not. I can't tell you how many times I heard my mother scold us: "Talk nice to each other. Be nice to your brother. Your words hurt your sister."

She was right. However, she didn't take her motherly advice far enough. Not only did we need to be challenged to speak kindly *to* each other, but we also should have been instructed to talk kindly *about* each other.

Recently my wife and I were at a gathering of friends. One couple in particular, David and Danielle, were very affectionate. Married five years, David was talking excitedly about how Danielle had just passed the bar exam and would be entering practice in the county prosecutor's office. He was obviously proud of her and her accomplishments, and she was grinning broadly, looking slightly embarrassed at his generous praise.

At first I thought nothing of what was happening, and then I began watching David more closely. He seemed to gain excitement the more he talked about how hard Danielle worked in law school, how she had achieved high marks even while raising their two preschool children, and how she had passed the exam on her first attempt.

Danielle, surprisingly, did little of the talking. She acknowledged that the exam had been difficult and admitted that law school had been challenging. But she stepped back, allowing her husband to freely champion her.

Did David gain points in his love bank? You'd better believe it. However, I'd be willing to bet that something else critical happened: *his estimation of her also grew the more he bragged about her.*

In the last chapter, we talked about the power of bringing out the best in your mate. In this chapter, I want to suggest another way to do this: positive gossiping. It's also the tenth step in becoming soul mates. More than anyone else, we must shout the praises of the one we were set on earth to be a helpmate to—our mate.

## Idle Gossip

We often consider gossiping a fault. Gossip is defined as spreading negative, unverifiable, and defamatory information about another person. It's easy to fall into spreading juicy tidbits—or criticizing others—safely out of their earshot, never considering the possible damage it might do.

There's no doubt gossip is big business in our society. We hunger after gossip about celebrities; it's no surprise that the TV show *Gossip Girls* inspired by a best-selling series of novels of the same name, is so popular.

The apostle Paul was concerned about gossip and dissension. Paul received reports that the church was killing its wounded. They were devouring one another with harsh, caustic words of gossip. As a body of believers, they were undoubtedly doing what we do today—chipping away at one another, little by little.

In his letter to the church at Philippi, Paul pleaded with two women, Euodia and Syntyche, "to agree with each other in the Lord" (Philippians 4:2). He later tells the church, "Whatever is true, whatever is noble, whatever is right, whatever is pure, whatever is lovely, whatever is admirable—if anything is excellent or praiseworthy—think about such things" (Philippians 4:8).

Can't you hear it in everyday English?

"Women! Stop the bickering. I'm tired of hearing it and it's pulling us down. And the rest of you: let's make a deal. If you don't have something nice to say, don't say anything. Let's build one another up, not tear each other down. Everything you say and do affects the other. We're a team. We're a family. C'mon. Let's pull together. I want to replace gossiping with positive comments. Notice the good things about each other and spread the good word."

Nothing weakens the effectiveness of a church, or any organization for that matter, more than being at odds with one another. The problem of gossip became very personal for Pastor Kevin Hester of the Sanctuary Baptist Church in Coloma, Michigan. After becoming the recipient of malicious gossip, he waged a campaign against it. Hester and his church have distributed two thousand "Gossip Free" bracelets, as well as a booklet called *Gossip Free? The High Cost of Low Talk* that Hester wrote. He is challenging people to go for eight days without gossiping or listening to gossip. Already people are noticing the positive difference.[1]

There is no question that gossip is often destructive, spoken against in Scripture, and antithetical to godly principles of healthy communication. But we can take the common human trait of sharing information and turn it into something wonderful.

## Positive Gossip

In World War II American fliers were given a can of shark repellent to use if they were shot down over the ocean. If that happened, they were to immediately open the can of repellent, which formed a protective barrier around them. As long as they had the protective repellent, they were safe. If they failed to use the repellent, they were vulnerable to shark attack.

In many ways you need a "shark repellent" to protect you and your spouse from gossip. Your "repellent" is Scripture, which teaches us to speak only what is true, what is noble, and what is right (Philippians 4:8).

While gossiping and the rumor mill can be ruinous, they do have something in common with what I am strongly promoting in this chapter—positive gossiping.

What exactly is positive gossiping? Positive gossiping is talking favorably about someone—in this case your mate—and letting that information spread like wildfire. I want you to positively gossip about your mate. I want people to hear, understand, amplify, and voraciously spread the good news about him or her.

Positive gossiping isn't really anything new—you know it as encouragement. I cannot advocate encouragement too strongly. Over my thirty-plus years of working with people, I'm still shocked at how dried and shriveled our spirits are, how hungry we are to be encour-

### GO AHEAD AND BRAG
Though bragging about ourselves can leave us feeling empty and embarrassed, bragging about our spouses brings us renewed joy and energy.

aged. Few of us feel that we receive enough. Want to really encourage your spouse? Discover a vulnerability in your mate, a place where he or she may feel insecure and build your spouse up in that area. Tell your spouse he or she can do it. Remind your mate of a time he or she has overcome a similar problem in the past; they can do it again.

But I want to offer a new, powerful twist to encouragement—public encouragement. Say something positive about your mate that you hope will spread! Champion your mate in front of others. Let others know some of the great things your mate is doing and how good you feel about it.

This may not come easily at first. We're not used to thinking in positive terms, and we're certainly not used to publicly encouraging others. We're much more comfortable offering criticism. When we do muster a compliment, or words of encouragement, there is often a barb attached.

"Your hair looks much nicer today."

"Thank you for that compliment. You never say anything nice about me."

"Thanks for the help. I don't know why it's so hard for you to give it."

"It's about time you gave me a helping hand."

Ouch. Offering compliments isn't something most of us are familiar with. We rarely practice it, and yet it can have a dramatic impact on our relationships.

Sharing compliments about our mates with others is critical to bringing out their best. As hard as it is to praise our mates directly, it seems even more awkward to say nice things about them to others.

It's not really as hard as it at first sounds. Let me try it, referencing my wife, Christie:

"You should see some of the great artwork my wife created in her interior design classes. It's incredible."
"You won't believe how fast Christie's peanut butter cake was eaten at the birthday party last night."
"Christie has become such a good editor of my books."
"Christie makes our home so pleasant and inviting."

Several nights ago we went out to dinner with friends and acquaintances to celebrate a birthday. When I was asked what I did, I explained that I was a psychologist and writer. People wanted to hear about my writing. I explained the kinds of books I wrote and then made a special effort to engage in positive gossiping.

"I used to hire a professional editor," I said. "But then I discovered that Christie does an excellent job of editing and enjoys doing it, so now she edits all my work."

"Is it tough to have your wife critique your work?" a woman asked.

I said, "Yes, to be honest it is hard at times. There is usually a bit of red ink on the page. She writes 'huh' and 'awk' in places that need work. But she puts lots of smiley faces on the places that she likes."

"That still must be challenging," the woman persisted.

"Yes," I said. "But Christie is always quick to tell me, 'Your work has good bones. With a little bit of work it can be a great chapter.'"

By this point in the conversation Christie was smiling, obviously enjoying the discussion. She felt appreciated, proud not only of her work, but also of the fact that I was bragging to other people about her. I snagged a fabulous opportunity to strengthen our marriage. Notice, however, that for my bragging to be helpful, my comments had to be specific and honest.

How tough was it to brag on her? Awkward at first, but it's become easier the more I do it. How about you? Can you think of things you

---

**PUBLIC DISPLAY OF AFFECTION**
You have more power than anyone else to build your mate's confidence and self-respect. You exercise this power whenever you praise your spouse to others in front of him or her.

---

could say about your mate, perhaps things he or she does to make your life easier or that make you proud?

Assume that your mate needs encouragement. Assume that your sincere praise will bring a smile to your spouse's face and draw you closer.

## Enrollment

One of my favorite books, which I return to again and again, is *The Art of Possibility*. This book by Rosamund Stone Zander and

Benjamin Zander is filled with possibility and encouragement. Rather than viewing the world from a place of scarcity and limitations, the authors see the world as filled with opportunity.

The Zanders discuss a concept that fits in beautifully with many of the themes in this book, including bringing out the best in your mate, the ripple effect, and nurturing each other's dreams. They call their idea *enrollment*.

Enrollment, as the Zanders explain, is not about forcing, cajoling, tricking, or pressuring someone into doing things your way. It is, rather, "the art and practice of generating a spark of possibility for others to share."[2]

The Zanders explain how in the Middle Ages people often carried around a metal box (tinderbox) containing a smoldering cinder, kept burning throughout the day with little bits of kindling. People could light a fire with ease, at any time, because they carried a spark with them wherever they went.

While the Zanders use this notion of enrollment in terms of sharing a contagious idea, I want to extrapolate their principle to the art of *enrolling others into appreciating the positive qualities of your mate*. Let's relate the Zanders' four steps on practicing the art of enrollment to passing on your excitement about your mate to others.

1. *Imagine that people are open to enrollment.* Expect that others are receptive to hearing exciting, positive information about your mate.
2. *Be willing to be moved and inspired by your mate.* As you listen to your spouse and interact with him or her on a daily basis, prepare yourself to be excited about his or her life and then share this excitement with others.
3. *Offer that which lights you up.* Having been inspired by your mate, you'll be unable to keep your excitement to yourself. It's like discovering an incredible idea—you want to share it with others. Having *caught* your mate's excitement, you'll want to pass it on.
4. *Have no doubt that others are eager to catch the spark.* Inspired and excited, you expect others not only to be eager listeners to what you have to say about your mate, but excited to pass

that spark along to others. Everyone wants something positive to cheer about.

What would happen if we each carried a tinderbox containing a spark of enthusiasm and excitement regarding our mates? What if we were ready, at all times, to share our wonderful feelings about our mates? This spark would warm us, spread to others, and then renew the warmth in our relationships.

## Showing Up Prepared

Like those in the Middle Ages who carried a tinderbox, kindling in hand, always ready to ignite a fire, the power of positive gossiping works best when you prepare yourself to send out sparks about your mate. You do this by thinking about the positive aspects of your mate so that when the opportunity arrives, you have something positive ready to say.

In her book *Brag!*, Peggy Klaus explains how the concept of promotion plants seeds for the future. While she is primarily talking about self-promotion, these same principles work magnificently when promoting others, especially your mate.

In talking about self-promoters, she says, "They're always planting seeds for the future. . . . Smart self-promoters show up prepared. They value face time with others and are always ready with stories about themselves that break through the verbal clutter. They know that positive regard from others isn't going to 'just happen.'"[3]

The parallel between promoting yourself and promoting your spouse is unmistakable. And while Klaus bemoans the fact that "the road traveled by a lackluster self-promoter is paved with missed opportunities,"[4] the same is certainly true of "mate-promotion." We miss so many opportunities to share with others what excites us about our mates.

Much of what I'm saying may sound incredibly foreign. Talk positively about our wives or husbands? Spread the good word about their job promotion, their impact as a parent, the way they tenderly care for an elderly parent? This is strange stuff—but, oh, so powerful.

To be prepared, of course, means we must truly know our mates.

This is no small matter. To be prepared to talk about them, to enthuse about them, to share what is keenly important to them, we must know them. We must know what burns in their hearts. We must know their wildest dreams. We must keenly listen, take notes, and be prepared to spread the good word about them.

---

### A WIN-WIN SITUATION
When you praise your spouse in front of other people, not only will their opinion of him or her go up—yours will too.

---

Stephen Covey espouses a critically important principle that underlies what I am saying about positive gossiping: *seek first to understand and then to be understood.* In other words, to be fully prepared to positively gossip about our mates we must truly know about their lives.

In *The 7 Habits of Highly Effective People*, Covey writes: "'Seek first to understand' involves a very deep shift in paradigm. We typically seek first to be understood. Most people do not listen with the intent to understand; they listen with the intent to reply. They're either speaking or preparing to speak. They're filtering everything through their own paradigms, reading their autobiography into other people's lives."[5]

In his follow-up best seller, *The 8th Habit*, Covey writes about the importance of each of us discovering our voice. While I agree that this is critical, I believe each of us discovering our mate's voice is equally critical. Championing his or her cause will bind our hearts to one another in a profound way.

In one of his first discourses, the Sermon on the Mount, Jesus told his followers that they were the salt of the earth, the light of the world (Matthew 5:13-16). He challenged them to live up to their true identity. Losing your saltiness (i.e., your distinctiveness) is not good for anyone. Hiding your light under a bowl doesn't shed light for others. The same is true for our mates. We must encourage them to be exactly who they were called to be, guarding their authenticity.

What would happen if we each had a positive story ready to share about something magnificent our mates were doing? What if we were ready to share something wonderful he or she was doing in our marriage? At a minimum, these sparks of positivity would reverberate inside our brains, leaking out in positive behavior toward our mates. At the most, we'd be ready to share a story with listeners, who are ready to tell a story to listeners, who are ready to tell a story to listeners. Armed with a tinderbox, our spark could start a wildfire.

## Bragging Rights

It is common to brag about our accomplishments. I've been known, a time or two, to even embellish upon something I've done that was particularly noteworthy.

However, we're trained *not* to brag. We're soundly scolded for "tooting our own horn," and appropriately so. Braggarts are difficult to listen to. When we know someone is "full of hot air," we take what he or she has to say with a grain of salt. We check ourselves from rolling our eyes and letting out a huge sigh of disgust.

A few years ago Christie put on a party to which we invited acquaintances from the business community. While we knew there would be schmoozing and socializing, we weren't quite prepared for the bragging of one guest.

This gentleman, whom we'll call Gene, came ready to sell us everything from his newly formed limousine service to his multilevel marketing plan involving kitchen products.

A tall, handsome man dressed for success in a dark blazer and slacks, Gene was pushy and borderline obnoxious. He seemed able to talk about only one subject—himself.

I watched Gene work the party. Business cards in hand, he made his multilevel marketing company sound like a straight shot at winning the lottery.

"You can't lose," he enthused. "These products sell themselves. You don't have to do anything to get product to fly off your shelves. I guarantee you'll be making six figures in six months, no question."

I watched Gene interact with our other guests, noticing as each politely listened and then tried to get away from him as quickly as possible. He couldn't see the impact he was having on those around him. His self-promotion had the opposite effect than he had hoped.

Just when I was ready to write Gene off, I saw something startling. Gene's wife, Mary, came alongside him and put her arm gently around his neck, as if to say, "It's okay. I'm here now. You're my hero." She smiled up at him and he smiled down at her.

In a dramatic act of gallantry, Gene turned toward his wife and looking at her said, "I'd like you to meet the most important person in my life. This is Mary, and she makes our house run smoothly, keeps my ego in check, picks up the pieces I drop all over the place, and has her own career as a teacher. She's the best."

Holy cow! I couldn't believe what I had seen and heard. Right in the middle of promoting his limousine service and multilevel marketing plan, Gene had dropped everything to put first things first. He had a promotional speech prepared about his wife, allowing her to bask in the limelight of his obvious affection for her.

I watched as the couple Gene had been talking to turned their attention to Mary. I watched her blush with satisfaction, drawing Gene even closer. The man and woman then turned their attention to Mary as Gene had the presence of mind to pull back and allow her to talk about her life as a mother, wife, and teacher.

My estimation of Gene, of course, went straight up. He not only was able to brag about himself, but he showed an uncanny ability to brag about his wife. He gossiped about what a wonderful woman she was and how lucky he was to have her. This was positive gossiping in action.

## Letting the Abundance Flow

In her best-selling book *Simple Abundance*, Sarah Ban Breathnach touts the benefits of authenticity. She also discusses the impact of those we admire on what we become: "Whom do you admire? If you tell me whom you admire, I could probably tell you a great deal about your hopes, dreams, and personal style."[6]

In other words, who we admire and who we think about reveal a great deal about us. I agree with Breathnach. The qualities you admire in your mate reveal much about you. If, on the other hand, you're stuck rehearsing the qualities you don't admire about your mate, that says something about you as well.

Undoubtedly you admire much about your mate—you wouldn't have married him or her if you didn't. While some of that admiration may have grown a bit dusty over the years, I suspect it's still there, perhaps hidden from sight. For as much as you might regret some of the negative aspects of your relationship, there are still qualities that can be pulled out, shined up, and reviewed to strengthen your marriage.

Who among us does not glow under the light of admiration? Who doesn't appreciate being admired for who he or she truly is? I so enjoy it when my wife walks up to me in a crowd and lets everyone know I'm her man. I know she appreciates when I do the same for her.

Positive gossiping will require you to shake off the cobwebs and rediscover the admiration you feel for your mate. It involves remembering why you married him or her, why you've stayed together, as well as what you still admire about him or her today.

There is plenty of love to go around if we will only loosen up and start sharing. We need only to draw upon our positive memories, giving ourselves permission to let the good words begin.

Scripture talks more about abundance than about scarcity. Just as God shares his abundance with us, I suggest we share our abundance with others—especially our mates. We have the opportunity, every day, to share abundantly *with* our mates and *about* our mates.

As Jesus says, "Give, and it will be given to you. A good measure, pressed down, shaken together and running over, will be poured into your lap. For with the measure you use, it will be measured to you" (Luke 6:38). Can you sense the movement in this passage? Give, and it will be given to you. How you give is how you will receive. Those are important lessons.

While we're tempted to read this Scripture as a promise about material wealth, I believe it really concerns our attitude toward others. Christ tells us we must be careful about how we view and treat others. Both should spring from an attitude of abundance. We must be patient, merciful, and loving, always ready to share our gratitude for our mates with others.

Sadly, too many of us are misers. We don't feel a sense of abundance, don't revel in our plentitude, and thus are reluctant to share the good qualities of our mates with others. It's like we're hoarding our good feelings, keeping them covered like the light under a bowl.

Julia Cameron writes at length about abundance and the importance of passing along love. She challenges us to let go of our miserly

---

**PLAN TO GOSSIP**
Think often about the positive aspects of your
spouse. That way, when the opportunity arises,
you'll have something positive ready to say.

---

attitude and give to ourselves, our mates, and others in abundance. "When we put a stopper on our capacity for joy by anorectically declining the small gifts of life, we turn aside the larger gifts as well."[7]

This quote gave me pause. I had to sit back and decide if I was adequately passing along the love I feel for my wife. Do I show her how much I love her? Do I share with others what Christie means to me? Too often I'm afraid, I don't. But the measure with which I give of myself is the measure by which I will receive.

## "I've Heard So Much about You"

My wife recently completed her degree in interior design. I had the pleasure of attending her graduation. There, amidst the cacophony of people, food, and music, were people I had never met but had heard so much about: the stiff, tightly wired professor who taught the history of furniture; the quirky, lovable professor of residential design; the students—some immediately likable, others anxious without a job in sight; still others quite caught up in a newfound sense of importance.

It was delightful to meet the people Christie had talked about for the past few years. She wanted me to meet them sooner, but there had been no opportunity. Here we were, years later, finally meeting.

"I've heard so much about you," one Asian man said. "So you're a psychologist? And you write too?" he asked. We struck up a lively conversation.

"I've heard so much about you," a vivacious, friendly woman said. "I'm a student here with Christie. She says such nice things about you."

"I've heard so much about you," a young man said. "Christie says you're a writer. Tell me about what you write."

Here I was, ready to champion Christie on her day, and these people I had never met were treating me like a celebrity. Christie had been talking. She had been sharing about our lives—she had been positively gossiping about me.

As the moments sped by, I felt a warm and powerful connection to Christie. She had been taking me to school with her. I was reminded that I was in her thoughts and her heart. She didn't forget about me when she was away from me, and these people reminded me of that.

"I've heard so much about you."

I hope you hear that statement from those in your mate's circle of friends. I also hope you share some wonderful things about your mate with others, so they can say the same when they meet your mate. You'll love the feeling you get when you hear it—and as you watch your spouse hear it. It's a win-win situation leading to a deeper bond as soul mates.

## Weekly Quiz

Sharing positive information about your mate may not come naturally, and will, in fact, take a little work. Are you ready to practice positive gossiping?

How might you handle the following situation:

You're having lunch with friends. One of them says, "You must be getting awfully tired of putting up with a spouse who works such long hours." You reply,

a) "You are so right. I've had it up to here," and then you continue bad-mouthing your mate.

b) "He and I have an understanding about the hours he is putting in right now. In fact, he is planning a special weekend away for us to celebrate the end of this project."

## PUTTING IT INTO PRACTICE THIS WEEK

1. If your spouse is discouraged about something this week, consider how you might either build him or her up in this area or express your unconditional love no matter what the outcome.

2. Does the idea of being ready with "good gossip" about your spouse seem contrived to you? If so, think about how easy it is to praise the accomplishments or efforts of a child in your life. Why is it so much harder to compliment your life partner?

3. Look for an opportunity to praise your spouse to someone else this week. It doesn't have to be anything big—for instance, if you grocery shop together and the cashier notes how much you were able to save on your bill with coupons, you might say something like, "Isn't it great? My wife [or husband] has a real knack for helping our family save money." You may feel self-conscious doing so at first; however, after the conversation, think about how you feel. If your spouse witnessed the exchange, talk about how he or she felt.

# INITIATING CHANGE
# BY ENCOURAGEMENT

*There are high spots in all of our lives and most of them come about through
encouragement from someone else. I don't care how great, how famous
or successful a man or woman may be, each hungers for applause.*

—George M. Adams

## SIGNS THAT YOU NEED TO INITIATE CHANGE BY ENCOURAGEMENT

1. You're much more likely to notice and comment when your spouse *doesn't* do the dishes than when he or she *does*.
2. When you enter the front door after work, even the dog finds someplace to hide.
3. You think it's important to tell it like it is.
4. Your spouse seems to shut down when you have an argument. (That means you've won, right?)
5. When you and your spouse disagree, it's more important to you that you're right than that you work together to find a solution.

For several years I drove into the driveway just before dinnertime and, upon noticing my sons' bikes lying on the driveway, stormed into the house ready to scold them. Marching angrily up the steps, I would see even more things that irritated me: my tools were not properly put away, my sons' jackets were lying on the floor, and the jelly and peanut butter jars were left on the counter.

Before I reached my sons' rooms, they scurried for cover, knowing they were in trouble. They knew the drill—I would be furious, ready to review their list of infractions. Naturally they tried to avoid me. This rarely worked since I was on a search and destroy mission—find the enemy, punish them, and correct the situation.

After a particularly harsh series of these nasty encounters, my older son, Joshua, then fifteen, took me aside.

"Can I talk to you, Dad?" he said with fear in his eyes.

"Of course, Son," I said, perceiving myself the epitome of the sensitive father.

"You don't want us to have fun, do you?" he said, his eyes peering deep into mine.

I stared at him in disbelief. I couldn't believe what he was asking. Why would he ask such a preposterous question? Was he trying to manipulate me? Was this a joke? I wanted only good things for my two sons, Joshua and Tyson. I would do anything so they could have a better life.

"Why do you ask that?" I answered, feeling completely perplexed and a bit ashamed.

"Because the first thing you do when you come home is find something to criticize. You're always mad, and Ty and I can't do anything right. You're always looking for something wrong and then jump on us about it. It doesn't make us want to improve things, that's for sure."

Stunned into silence and fighting back tears, I looked at him. Joshua was dead serious. This was his reality—a father who drove into the driveway with one purpose in mind, to find something wrong. And he always did.

My son's candor changed my life. His last words were the most dramatic, leaving a lasting memory—"It doesn't make us want to improve things, that's for sure."

What? That was the purpose, or so I thought, for my actions—to make my sons improve. To get them to stop leaving their bikes in the driveway, leaving their jackets on the floor, and forgetting to put the peanut butter and jelly away. I was trying to bring order to an apparently chaotic world.

But my actions didn't work. What did work, after I decided *my* life needed correcting, was completely changing my approach. I determined from that day forward to catch my sons doing things right. I would notice everything they did correctly and praise them for it. I would build them up instead of putting them down. The difference between criticism and encouragement was positively dramatic.

## Slipping into Criticism

Joshua displayed insight and maturity beyond his years. He knew intuitively about an important aspect in relationships. It is this aspect that forms the basis of our eleventh task in bringing out the soul mate in your mate: initiating change by encouragement.

Criticism can make us feel as if we're in control, and we may even insist we're offering it to help our spouse. Instead, criticism serves only to antagonize our mates. Criticism alienates, wounds, hurts, and

. . . . . . . . . . . . . . . . . . . . . . . . . . . . . . . . . . . . . . . . . . . . . . . . . . . . . . . . . . . . . . . . . . . .

**DESTRUCTIVE CRITICISM**
Criticism alienates, wounds, and aggravates.
It never motivates, heals, or resolves a problem.

. . . . . . . . . . . . . . . . . . . . . . . . . . . . . . . . . . . . . . . . . . . . . . . . . . . . . . . . . . . . . . . . . . . .

aggravates. It never heals or brings mates together to solve problems. While Joshua couldn't articulate the full impact of criticism, he was able to say, in his own way, "I don't like it."

Harville Hendrix, in his book *Keeping the Love You Find*, articulates what my son shared in his youthful words. "Criticism is the most common reaction to frustration in a relationship, and it is the most destructive, a perverse and counterproductive attempt to get one's needs met or to correct an uncomfortable situation. Its misguided premise is that if we inflict pain on another person, we can get him or her to relieve our pain, to be sorry for the hurt s/he caused us."[1]

Yes, that's it. I was frustrated, irritated, and angry. If I could punish Joshua and Tyson enough, I was certain they would change and all my bad feelings would disappear. But, as Hendrix says, that doesn't work.

Just as surely as criticism found its way into my relationship with my sons, it crept into my first marriage as well. I criticized my wife when I was angry with her, hoping she would change. Criticism, however, only served to do what it did to my sons—push her away.

I shouldn't be surprised that I'm prone to criticize—we're all prone to slipping into this unbelievably bad habit. Criticism is everywhere, especially in our most intimate and personal relationships. Where we expect to find love and generosity—with our soul mates—too often we find negativity, harshness, and criticism.

Why is it so tempting to offer criticism when we know intellectually that encouragement is more effective? What is it about criticism that makes it so tempting to use, even with the person we love? Consider these ideas:

*Criticism is reinforced in our society.* Everywhere I turn I hear people criticizing someone for something. I notice couples criticizing one another for how they dress, the way they discipline their children, the amount of money they spend, and myriad other issues. Blame and criticism are rampant, learned and then repeated in our marriages.

*But you're going to break this trend through initiating change by encouragement!* You're going to eradicate criticism from your marriage. Soul mates have compassion and understanding for one another. They realize that encouragement, rather than criticism, warms the heart. They accept, embrace, and even celebrate differences rather than force their spouses to bend to their wishes and whims.

*Criticism occurs naturally when we interact closely with others.* Wherever there are two people, there will be two different opinions, two different points of view, and two different histories. With these differences, there will often be conflict and criticism of the other's point of view. This is to be expected.

*But you're going to break this trend through initiating change by encouragement!* You're going to expect tension at times, tolerate it, and remind yourself that differences are inevitable. You'll remember that different points of view add texture and variety to a marriage. You're going to remind yourself there is no *right* point of view, and that there are as many points of view as there are people.

*Criticism makes us feel powerful.* Armed with a feeling of righteous indignation, we feel powerful when we criticize each other. Often when we believe we're in the *right*, we feel little guilt or remorse about our behavior. In fact, we feel stronger when we blame and attack. We feel justified in pushing our will onto someone else.

*But you're going to break this trend through initiating change by encouragement!* Soul mates don't succumb to these insecure maneuvers to feel strong and powerful. They find security in legitimate ways, by being kind and caring, sensitive and thoughtful. They realize encouragement is a far greater motivator than criticism.

Criticism is not only unproductive, it's wrong. The apostle James says we argue and criticize because we don't have what we want, and we selfishly go after it. We criticize in order to get our own, selfish way (James 4:1-2).

*Criticism is our attempt at perfection.* Critics are continuously trying to make things turn out a certain way. They want things the way they want them. They want to "win." They have an image of how things *ought* to be and are determined to force things to fit into their vision.

This kind of perfectionism is, of course, stifling. To live with a perfectionist is to always feel as if you never measure up. To live with a perfectionist is to forever feel pushed, pulled, maneuvered, and possibly even manipulated.

*But you're going to break this trend through initiating change by encouragement!* You're going to celebrate a bit of messiness. You're

......................................................................

**THE PITFALL OF PERFECTIONISM**
Critics believe they know how things ought to be and
are determined to force things to fit their vision.

......................................................................

going to have fun with differences and know everything won't always turn out the way you'd like in a perfect world. You're going to have fun with life's curveballs!

Thomas Moore talks extensively about the messiness of soulful living—the goal of soul mates. "When we shift our attention from the mechanics and structures of a relationship to its soul, a number of changes occur. . . . We can find some purpose in the failures, the intimacies that never got off the ground, the possibilities that never took flesh. The soul does not share the spirit's love of perfection and wholeness, but finds value in fragmentation, incompleteness, and unfulfilled promise."[2]

Soul mates accept the differences between them, agreeing with Moore that these dissimilarities even spice up their marriage. A little "messiness" is good for the soul and good for soul mates. Today's troubles are tomorrow's stories and encouragement around the campfire. Today's challenges are tomorrow's celebrations and proof that you made it through in one piece to tell about it.

## Even Soul Mates Have Squabbles

Oh, how I wish it weren't so. I wish I could promise you that the Land of Soul Mates is the closest thing to the Garden of Eden this side of heaven. I want to tell you that by practicing the tools offered in this book and by bringing out the soul mate in your mate, you'll be forever free of conflict. I really do want to say that to you. But it wouldn't be true. So back to reality.

Even soul mates have squabbles. Even soul mates slip into unhealthy criticisms and power struggles at times. But unlike those who don't work on creating a soul-mate marriage, they get out of squabbles nearly as fast as they get into them. They set boundaries on those struggles and never let them define their relationship.

Raised in a somewhat raucous family, where words were spilled out like water, I had grown accustomed to regular criticism. With four siblings, sarcasm was common and provocation an everyday occurrence. Later, while training to become a psychologist, I was taught to believe we should vent our pent-up emotion.

I'm now unsure of that counsel. I've learned that criticism doesn't feel good. I've never learned to like it or even appreciate it. Constructive or not, I don't like it. Even if it is meant to help me grow and become a better person, I still don't like it. Too often it cuts and hurts.

Is there a place for criticism with soul mates? While I believe soul mates can and will be critical of each other, their relationship will not be defined by criticism. They will not be preoccupied with attempts to control and change their mates. They will live by a spirit of cooperation and encouragement rather than a spirit of frustration and criticism.

Soul mates are truthful with each other, but they are not critical. They have learned the fine art of being honest without tearing down their mates. They know that issues must be addressed, and truth must

................................................................................

## SOUL MATES *DO* SQUABBLE
Even the closest spouses will disagree and sometimes wound one another. However, they're quicker than other couples in recognizing the disconnection and working through divisive issues.

................................................................................

be spoken. They practice the biblical model of love which "rejoices in the truth" (1 Corinthians 13:6, NKJV).

Recently I asked Christie for feedback on an article I had written. She could tell I was tentative about receiving her feedback. As she read the article, however, she saw several areas that could be strengthened. While I wanted to know the *truth* about my writing, she knew I didn't want to be criticized. We are learning how to walk that fine line.

"You made a lot of really good points," she said. I waited for the rest of the story. "You can strengthen your article by tightening up this section," she said pointing to a particular paragraph, "and by adding more detail to this story."

"That's it?" I asked, expecting worse.

"Do that and it'll be perfect," she said, smiling.

I paused, looking at her. She had offered criticism without being critical. She had given me feedback in a way that didn't attack me as a person. She made no global criticism, no derogatory comments, only *suggestions that I was free to accept or reject.* I felt free to consider what she said and free to do what I wanted to do. Trusting her invaluable expertise, I chose to attend to her suggestions.

Soul mates learn to guard their tongues and give criticism carefully, with heavy doses of encouragement. Soul mates *never* do anything to intentionally harm their mates. When something *must* be said that has the potential to harm, they use tact, couching their words so as to build their mates up.

## The Power of Encouragement

Soul mates learn to initiate change through encouragement rather than attempting to fix things through criticism. Criticism is an ineffective method for enacting change. No one wants to be criticized. Criticism leaves us feeling demoralized, discouraged, and detached from one another. Criticism makes us want to withdraw, while encouragement pulls us closer to one another, motivating us to put forth our best. Encouragement has always been a potent motivator and is naturally used by soul mates.

Jenn and Carl were locked in a power struggle when they came to see me. Jenn, a slender forty-year-old dressed in jeans and sweatshirt, quickly announced she had significant doubts as to her husband's ability to change. Her forceful and angry spirit was immediately obvious.

"What is the change you're after?" I asked as we began our session.

"I want to be able to meet with my friends without Carl feeling threatened," she said. "I'm not doing anything wrong. It's ridiculous that he feels threatened."

Carl, dressed in khakis and a sport shirt, sat quietly, tapping his fingers on the chair as he waited for his turn to talk.

"Look," he said slowly. "I love my wife. I want her to spend time with me, not the friends she goes to coffee shops with. What's wrong with spending evenings with me instead of them?"

Jenn bristled, turning her head away.

In a just a few short moments, I could see Jenn and Carl were locked in a power struggle. They addressed each other as adversaries instead of teammates. Their voices belied anger rather than humility, coercion rather than cooperation.

A few minutes of exploration revealed that Jenn and Carl had been married twenty years and had two grown children. While their marriage was stable, they had bumped into an issue that was dividing them. Jenn now wanted to spend more time with friends—not to the exclusion of Carl, but in addition to spending time with him.

Carl felt threatened by Jenn's new behavior, but rather than brainstorm solutions with her, he spoke harshly about her new friends, criticizing her motives as well as her behavior. He tried to point out that she was wrong, while he was right. This led to Jenn becoming stubborn, pushing away from Carl, refusing to even negotiate.

After listening to the sharp exchange between them, I asked, "Is this what happens at home?"

"Only when this topic comes up," Jenn said, smiling. "Otherwise, we get along great and really love each other. This topic brings us to an immediate boil."

"I don't think the issue is your friends, but rather how you talk about this issue. I'm going to offer some drastic ideas for changing how you think about this problem, how you talk about it, and how you find solutions. Are you both open to exploring some new ways of thinking about this?" I asked.

Both agreed to listen.

As Carl and Jenn stepped back from the issue, they were able to soften their defensive demeanor toward each other. They were ready to listen to, to learn, and to understand their mate's position. They were ready to shift from being enemies to being partners. We could now begin finding a solution that worked for them both.

## When We Simply Must Say Something

Before summarizing the guidelines I gave them, let me acknowledge that there will be times when we feel compelled to offer an opinion. When we feel we're on the side of the "right" and want to make our point, we nearly cannot stop ourselves from voicing our opinions. I appreciate that and again want to offer some thoughts to help you navigate this sticky arena.

There are times when you simply must say something about your mate's behavior. You've tried encouragement, and their irresponsible behavior continues. You've tried speaking the truth in love, and still agreements are broken. You've got to say something.

Giving critical feedback is as much an art as a science. Being attuned to our mates, particularly their strengths and vulnerabilities, is crucial when offering feedback. Some people like critical feedback offered directly, while others, like me, like the gentle, tactful approach. Some want feedback any time you want to give it. Others, like me, want it only at certain times, when they feel on top of their game. Knowing your mate, and his or her style, is very important when saying something delicate.

As we prepared to talk about their power struggle in a new and different way, I gave Jenn and Carl some basics on how to offer critical feedback, which you may also find helpful:

1. *Your mate is much more likely to welcome your feedback when it is given from an open heart and generosity of spirit.* When your mate believes you are coming to him or her with a concern of simply wanting to get your own way, he or she will naturally close down and put up barriers to communication. If, on the other hand, he or she is convinced that you are sharing something for the good of the relationship, your feedback is generally much better received.

   Author Stephanie Dowrick says, "Generosity builds human spirit. Every act of generosity—the willing giving of your time, interest, concern, care, understanding, humor, loyalty, honesty—expresses and nourishes love. And every missed opportunity to be generous erodes your experience of love, connectedness and spirit."[3]

2. *Remind your mate that you come to him or her with a concern because you want to strengthen your relationship.* Soul mates know they must come to the bargaining table motivated by a desire to improve their marriage. So, when bringing a concern to your mate, don't come ready to manipulate, coerce, or get your own way. The focus should not be on changing your mate but on sharing his or her vulnerabilities. Come to your spouse from the position of wanting to find a solution that works for you both.

3. *Focus on specific issues.* Rather than make global complaints, soul mates address specific issues. They take one issue at a time and avoid making generalizations.

   John Gottman, who outlined groundbreaking research in the book *Why Marriages Succeed or Fail,* found that global criticisms were one of four fatal horsemen in marriages that failed. "Criticism involves attacking someone's personality or character—rather than a specific behavior—usually with blame."[4] Blame is devastating to a marriage.

Let's say you and your spouse agree that he or she will go out and buy a new floor lamp for the living room. If your mate comes home with one that cost twice as much as you agreed upon, you certainly have a right to express your disappointment. As a soul mate, you offer a specific complaint: "I am upset that you didn't keep your agreement about spending no more than a hundred dollars."

4. *Focus on specific solutions.* This is where soul mates shine! They are positive and solution-focused. This is how it might work for you: After letting your spouse know you are upset that he or she spent too much, you might say: "I want to renew our agreement that when one of us goes shopping without the other we will stick to the amount of money we budgeted to spend on that item." By keeping things simple, you increase the possibility of receiving a positive response. Soul mates don't care to dredge up what happened last year or figure out who's more right or wrong. Soul mates want to solve problems and get on with loving and learning.

Soul mates never make global attacks, judging motives and vilifying character, but rather they make specific requests.

5. *Treat mistakes as part of a learning curve, not the end of the world.* Soul mates are secure in each other's love and subsequently don't freak out when a mistake is made. They address the mistake, learn from it, and get on with things. Rather than getting bogged down in a problem, they simply regroup, review their agreements, and make a more concerted effort to keep them.

If you or your spouse believe an agreement you've made with one another has been repeatedly violated or that one of you consistently disregards the thoughts and feelings of the other, look for the deeper issue involved. Perhaps one partner made an agreement he or she doesn't really want to keep. Perhaps one of you needs to address a more pervasive character issue. Even mistakes and broken agreements can be viewed as an opportunity to look a bit closer at the relationship.

    6. *Notice and encourage positive movement.* Soul mates are always catching each other doing things right. They recognize progress and make a big deal about it. No one wants to feel as though his or her efforts aren't being recognized, so be generous with your praise and admiration.

Remember the story in the beginning of the book about teaching a chicken to dance? Let's consider this illustration again, especially as it applies to the art of offering critical feedback. Remember, it's absolutely true that you can teach a chicken to dance—under the right circumstances. Should you decide to give it a try, follow these four steps:
    First, reinforce the chicken every time it approximates doing the right dance step.
    Second, keep reinforcing the chicken every time it approximates doing the right dance step.
    Third, don't kick the chicken in the head when it makes a mistake.
    Fourth, keep reinforcing the chicken every time it approximates doing the right dance step.
    Enjoy the dancing chicken.
    Hopefully you can see the parallel between teaching a chicken to dance and strategies for offering critical feedback! Encouragement is paramount; discouragement, punishment, blame, and criticism don't work!

## Kicking Blame Out the Door

Blame and encouragement have a very hard time living together. Blame finds faults, while encouragement finds victories. Blame pulls down, while encouragement builds up. They really cannot live in the same house, so you're going to have to make a decision about who stays and who goes.
    Blame is our futile attempt to affix responsibility onto someone.

Soul mates don't need to do this and will instead give up this vain attempt to control a situation. Soul mates don't try to alleviate their responsibility by forcing their spouses to see how wrong and bad they are. Blame has never worked and never will.

Consider the adverse effects of blame:

*Blame* says you're the one at fault.
*Encouragement* says we are both engaging in actions that contribute to the problem.

*Blame* says you must change.
*Encouragement* says we must solve this problem together.

*Blame* is narrow minded.
*Encouragement* is open minded.

*Blame* is ego-driven.
*Encouragement* is Spirit-guided.

*Blame* says this problem is the end of the world.
*Encouragement* says this problem is an opportunity for growth.

*Blame* says we are adversaries.
*Encouragement* says we are a team and must work together to find a solution.

*Blame* says our relationship is all about this particular problem.
*Encouragement* says our relationship is bigger than this one, singular issue.

We can see the stifling impact of blame on Jenn and Carl. Jenn blames Carl for being narrow minded and unsympathetic. Angry at his efforts to control her and feeling smugly in the right, she refuses to budge.

Carl is stuck feeling righteously indignant. He emphatically believes Jenn's actions are wrong. Since he blames her for their problems, he gives little ground either.

Author Lewis Losoncy shares the beauty of what occurs with soul mates: "Once we stop blaming others, instead of judging them, we will sensitively listen to them to understand them more effectively from their vantage point."[5]

I immediately became aware that Jenn and Carl were stuck in the destructive pattern of blame. If they could not stop blaming each other they would remain stuck, and their marriage could be in jeopardy. If they could pull back, take a deep breath, and remember their love for each other, they could work together to find a solution to their problem.

## Receiving Critical Feedback with a Smile

If you thought giving critical feedback was tricky, try receiving it with a smile on your face. Believe me, it's tough! Nobody really likes it. No one wants to hear he or she has room to improve. But, again, we're not in Kansas anymore, Toto, so we've got to deal with reality. Let's make sure we've got this part of soul-mate relating mastered.

The reality is that you're going to make mistakes. Nothing earth-shattering, we hope, but high enough on the Richter scale to come to the attention of your soul mate. How are you going to handle it when your mate addresses the problem? Will you get defensive, point the finger of blame back on him or her, and try to dodge responsibility? I certainly hope not.

Soul mates generally feel safe when giving or receiving critical feedback because they've agreed to kick blame out the door. They know criticism must be limited, and encouragement must be given regularly. They give up the need and desire to punish their mates for perceived or actual wrongdoing. They are more concerned with their relationship than with being right. Their marriages are enhanced because they rigorously ensure they keep problems in perspective and amplify the positive aspects of their union.

Still, every couple, including soul mates, needs to learn or renew strategies for receiving critical feedback, since this is perhaps the greatest area that can take a relationship south. If you don't know how to listen to your mate when he or she is annoyed, bugged, and generally discontent, you're in for a bumpy ride. So let's strap on our safety harness, buckle up that crash helmet, and learn how the pros handle conflict.

What follows are five tools—only five!—that you must review, rehearse, and remind yourself of again and again. Post these on the fridge and lovingly encourage your mate to practice these with you. Okay, here we go!

1. *Never defend yourself or debate with your mate.* Yes, I know this is incredibly counterintuitive, illogical, and, to some, nonsensical. Still, try it. When we defend ourselves, we are caught in a shame bind, according to John Bradshaw in his book *Healing the Shame That Binds You.* In other words, when you defend yourself, you're already hooked, hopelessly caught in a trap of trying to defend yourself while trying to get unhooked. Rather than throwing out a boatload of excuses, rationalizations, and perhaps even lies—which people tend to do when they get hooked—it's far better not to get hooked in the first place.

   How can you remain unhooked? You allow your mate to have an opinion, point of view, feelings, and beliefs. By being detached and unhooked, you can listen to your spouse dispassionately. You'll be in a far better place to hear the truth of what he or she is saying.

2. *Listen for a kernel of truth.* This leads nicely to your second tool. Own up to some part of what your mate is saying. Find the truth in his or her confrontation. Lean in. Face the music like a big boy or girl.

   When Carl criticized Jenn about staying out late with her friends, she could say, "Yes, you're right. I have stayed out late with my friends and that has upset you." Can you imagine the power of her statement? Carl sighs with relief as she acknowledges his feelings. Instead of locking horns and debating, she has agreed with him on a point. They're on their way to a healing agreement.

3. *Ask for clarification.* As you remain detached and listen for the kernel of truth in what your spouse is saying, you can

stay cool by asking for more information. Without defending yourself, probe for your mate's feelings. "What exactly is it that bothers you about what I've done?" Ask for very specific feedback. Work at getting to the heart of the matter, encouraging your mate to share his or her feelings.

Clarification between Jenn and Carl sounded like this: "Let me see if I get this right. You don't want me to visit with my friends because you're afraid I might make some foolish choices with men. Is that right?" Jenn's question encourages Carl to be clear about his concerns and allows Jenn time to consider where Carl is really coming from.

4. *When wrong, quickly confess your wrongful actions.* Rather than putting up a smoke screen or spitting back in defensiveness, admit wrongdoing. Confess your error and acknowledge the impact it has had on your mate.

   Confession has always been a powerful action that binds hearts together. Soul mates know they have nothing to lose by admitting they are sometimes wrong. Admitting wrongdoing doesn't lead to loss of ego—rather, it leads to growth and strengthening of both yourself and your relationship.

   Carl admitted he had been trying to make Jenn feel bad for her actions and apologized to her. Jenn admitted her rebelliousness and agreed to work with Carl to find a solution that worked for both of them.

5. *Offer to make amends, comforting your mate for your wrong actions.* As you actively listen, empathize with your mate and acknowledge any pain you inadvertently caused. Remind yourself that your mate is critical of a specific action, not your entire personhood. Then offer to make amends for what you've done, which is a way to acknowledge wrongdoing and indicate you are aware your actions have caused distress.

Carl and Jenn are well on their way to becoming soul mates. They are dedicated to practicing and mastering these five tools. However, they also realize progress is made one step at a time. Even soul mates criticize, squabble, and have occasional meltdowns. While soul mates practice calling time-out when things get heated and learn how to listen non-defensively, they realize the best-laid plans at times don't work out. But they also realize that when things don't work out, it's not the end of the world. It's a temporary, situation-specific mess-up. Should this happen to you and your mate, pick yourselves up, dust yourselves off, make appropriate apologies and amends, and get it behind you. Disagreements happen! A "do-over" is one of the most powerful tools in marriage.

## Being in Your Happy Place

Soul mates strive to remain in their happy place, because when they are happy, they are more likely to be happy and kind to their mates.

It's especially critical to be kind with your words. Although humans have impulses to say whatever is on their minds, soul mates guard their tongues, recognizing that any and every word spoken has the power to encourage or to tear down. There are no "slips of the tongue" because they know they cannot take back these slips. They have purposely dedicated their tongues and words to building up their mates.

Perhaps my favorite passage when counseling couples is Ephesians 4:29: "Do not let any unwholesome talk come out of your mouths, but only what is helpful for building others up according to their needs, that it may benefit those who listen."

This is such a powerful truth. What would happen if you dedicated yourself to saying *only* what would build up your mate? What if your words were guided by the directive that they were to benefit him or her? This means that *every word* is considered.

I am writing these words on a Saturday morning. It is a casual day in the Hawkins's home, with few obligations, little structure, and a carefree attitude. I love weekends. I am up early, and Christie is still sleeping.

Because I desire to be a soul mate, I'm thinking about how I will greet her when she walks sleepily into my office. Because I want to set a positive tone for our day and because I love her, I will greet her cheerfully. She will undoubtedly react cheerfully, and we'll start our day off right.

Every word, every encounter, every gesture we make will be either encouraging or discouraging, and that is why we must make every one of them count. The selfish ego or the generous Spirit will drive every action taken.

## Telling the Truth in Love

Soul mates keep one thing in focus at all times: their love for their partners. No matter what is happening, no matter how they feel at the moment, no matter what—they keep that love in the front of their minds. Every single word said must be said in love.

Carl had a thing or two to learn about this idea of focusing on being *lovingly* truthful.

...............................................................................

**TRY A LITTLE TENDERNESS**
Soul mates guard their tongues, recognizing that every word they speak will either encourage or tear down their mates.

...............................................................................

"But I only tell the truth," Carl said smugly. "I never lie, and I don't believe in beating around the bush."

"And you think that is a virtue?" I said. "Are you aware of the impact your words have on your marriage? Do you know how Jenn feels about your words?"

"That's not my responsibility," he said firmly. "How she takes it is up to her."

"That is only partially true, Carl," I replied, noting his rigid and defensive posture. I'd heard this argument—the importance of simply stating the truth—hundreds of times before.

Jenn appeared sad and withdrawn, tired from the months of arguing with Carl over this issue.

"What's wrong with what I'm saying?" Carl added, still bristling from his belief that he had a right to say anything he wanted as long as he deemed it truthful.

"First," I began, "we are not called simply to tell the truth, but to tell it in love. This means before speaking we test our words, considering whether the information will build up our mates. We also ask ourselves if any harm can come from what we're saying."

"Okay," he said slowly.

"Second," I continued, "we must recognize that what we're saying is *our version of the truth.* What you're saying would more accurately be called opinion or preference. You must leave Jenn room to see things differently than you. If you don't, she'll perceive you as dangerous and not looking out for her highest good. She'll also feel hemmed in and manipulated by your version of the truth, as if she has to buy it wholesale whether she likes it or not."

"I sort of get that," Carl said softly, "but it still seems like truth is truth."

"Sometimes," I conceded, "but more often than not, what you communicate as truth is simply your perception of the truth. My version won't necessarily fit with yours."

"Hmm," he said.

"I actually have a third thought, if you're willing to hear it," I said, trying to get Carl to budge.

"Sure," he said reluctantly.

"If we present our truth in an argumentative way, it leaves little *invitation* to share opposing beliefs and thoughts. The relationship shrivels and stifles rather than becoming larger with possibilities. Take me, for example. I want to talk with people who will honestly consider my point of view as I consider theirs. The conversation is open, flexible, freeing, and exciting with possibilities. That's the way soul mates relate, and I know you want that for you and Jenn."

"This is going to take some consideration," Carl said slowly. "I'm not used to thinking this way, but what you're saying makes sense. I do love Jenn and want her to feel safe with me."

"Actually, it works for me too," Jenn said. "Both Carl and I could stand to practice this. I think it would make a big difference in our marriage."

"So, Carl," I said smiling. "Do you want to give it a try? What is something you might say to Jenn that would be true for you, while making it clear that it is strictly your perception?"

"Okay," he said slowly. "Here goes. Jenn, there's nothing wrong with going out with your friends, but I'd like it if you spent a little less time away from home in the evenings and a bit more time with me. How's that?"

"That's a lot better, Carl," she said. "'A' for effort."

Soul mates tell the truth and rigorously ensure there are no secrets or deception in their relationship. But they're careful to maintain the bridge of rapport they've meticulously built. They know, oh so well, that a word misspoken can weaken this bridge.

If I've learned anything in my counseling experience, as well as my marriage, it's the importance of sharing what we think without offending each other. Since you've been fortunate enough to find love, you must protect it from everything that could erode it, including your words.

Genuine happiness comes from feeling unconditionally loved and loving other people. When both you and your spouse feel loved and cared for, you'll *want* to give your mate what he or she needs. You both will change willingly, perhaps even excitedly, knowing the change will please the other. Because you are feeling encouraged, rather than coerced, change occurs easily and naturally.

You've learned many powerful tools used by soul mates. You've learned the incredible power of encouragement and are now ready to ban blame and misspoken words from your marriage. You've tasted a bit of bringing out the best in your mate, and there is more to come. Each strategy is important, and building one upon another will form an incredible foundation for bringing out the soul mate in your mate.

We're ready to turn to the final chapter of the book—maintaining mutual admiration. Let's explore how soul mates sustain a loving, admiring relationship.

## Weekly Quiz

We know, intellectually, that criticism doesn't work well to change behavior. We all respond much more effectively to encouragement. Yet eradicating criticism from our marriages may be hard to do.

Consider how you might handle this situation:

Your mate walks through the door after work, tossing his coat over the back of the chair. You

a) forcefully remind him you've asked him a thousand times to stop throwing his coat on the chair and sarcastically suggest you are not his mother.

b) decide this is not the time or place to make an issue out of the coat. Instead, you choose to hang up the coat yourself and tell him you're glad he's home. You resolve to make a point of expressing your appreciation for hanging up the coat the next time he does so on his own.

. . . . . . . . . . . . . . . . . . . . . . . . . . . . . . . . . . . . . . . . . . . . . . . . . . . . . . . . . . . . . . . . . . . . . . . . . . . . .

## PUTTING IT INTO PRACTICE THIS WEEK

1. When we want our spouse to change, why is it generally easier to criticize than to encourage?

2. Is there an issue or problem that repeatedly causes tension and conflict between you and your mate? If so, set aside a half hour or so to take turns discussing it. When offering feedback to your spouse, remember to give feedback
   - that comes from an understanding heart and a generous spirit
   - that's designed to strengthen your relationship rather than prove you're right
   - that is specific
   - that recognizes any positive change you've observed

   When listening to feedback from your spouse, remember to
   - listen, not to debate or defend yourself
   - listen for the truth (even if it's just a kernel) in what they're saying
   - ask for clarification
   - acknowledge any hurt—intentional or not—you have caused your spouse

3. Seek to encourage your mate this week, pointing out the many things he or she does to contribute to your family and your marriage.

# MAINTAINING MUTUAL ADMIRATION

*In every sound and sight around my house, an infinite and unaccountable*
*friendliness, all at once, like an atmosphere, sustaining me.*
—Henry David Thoreau

## SIGNS THAT YOU NEED TO MAINTAIN MUTUAL ADMIRATION

1. The first time you try praising your spouse for a job well done, he or she pretends to think you've lost your mind . . . but kind of likes it.
2. "Of course I love you! I married you, didn't I?"
3. Love means never having to say you're sorry—unless your spouse ticks you off.
4. *You mean I have to keep doing this soul mate stuff? I thought this was just for 90 days!*
5. When your spouse says he or she wants to feel safe with you, your mind immediately goes to hard hats and protective goggles.

Yikes! Having spent the evening taking care of long overdue paperwork at my office, I arrived home two hours later than usual. I thought Christie was going to be out late, visiting her daughter in Seattle. My heart skipped a beat when I pulled into our driveway and noticed her car.

"What is her car doing here?" I mumbled to myself. My mind rushed through the possibilities. Had she hurried to Seattle and just arrived home? Had her plans fallen through, leaving her free for the evening? Or could it be worse—did I misunderstand her plans, and would I walk in the door to find our dinner, as well as her affections, cold?

As I walked up the steps, she opened the door. Then she greeted me with a warm embrace and soft kiss. Well, I couldn't be in too much trouble.

"Where have you been?" she asked, with a hint of impatience in her voice.

"I've been dillydallying at the office," I said. "Weren't you going to Seattle tonight?"

"No," she said. "Do you remember me telling you my plans had changed? I've been here. I expected you around six."

"I'm sorry," I explained, sharing with her my misunderstanding.

Throwing my sports coat onto a chair, I invited Christie to sit with me on the couch.

"So tell me how badly I've muffed this evening," I said apologetically.

"Well, I was going to go to Seattle to meet Kira but I was missing you, so I changed my mind. I told her, 'I want to be with my man!' She understood."

"Ouch," I said. I was already feeling bad. "Did you really say that?"

Christie grabbed my hand and said it again.

"I told her I wanted to be with my man tonight, and I still do."

She warmed up dinner and, more important, kept her heart warm for me as well. Talk about making a guy feel special. Christie had a choice to make—carry a grudge and create distance, or offer understanding and keep her flame of admiration alive. Thankfully for me, she chose the latter.

Our final and perhaps most potent strategy for bringing out the soul mate in our mates is maintaining mutual admiration. Even when circumstances create tension and potential distance, admiration is the bond that keeps romantic fires burning, respect alive and vibrant, and love dynamic.

## The Bond of Admiration

Admiration is a strong and enduring bond between people. It is the bridge that keeps relationships alive and strong when the chips are down. Admiration is a fragile bond that must be preserved and protected above all else.

M. C. Migel knew the power of admiration when he enlisted
Helen Keller's assistance in lobbying Congress in his attempt to per-
suade President Franklin Delano Roosevelt to approve funding of
Talking Book machines. As the president of the American Foundation for the Blind (AFB), Migel needed something done and looked
to the people he respected and admired to help him. Keller had earlier
asked Roosevelt, when he was governor of New York, to become an
honorary member of AFB.

Migel recognized an opportunity to get funding for the manufac-
ture of Talking Book machines through the Works Progress Adminis-
tration, which had been created by Roosevelt. To do so, he capitalized
on the warm relationship and mutual admiration that existed between
Keller and Roosevelt. He received the funding.

Mutual admiration has always fostered relationships, and thus its
power should cause us no surprise. Who doesn't want to be admired
and appreciated? When we feel appreciated, we want to be kind and
generous to those who appreciate us.

Surprisingly, we too quickly forget this principle. We behave as
if we can put someone down or ignore him or her one moment
and then ask for a helping hand the next. But this is not the way it
works. It's not the way of civility, and it's certainly not the way of
soul mates.

Consider some of these common platitudes:

- "One good turn deserves another."
- "You scratch my back and I'll scratch yours."
- "What you give is what you'll get."
- "Do unto others as you'd have them do unto you."

Again, this is not rocket science. These are basic principles of relating. We must critically examine how we treat our mates, not only
because it is the right thing to do, but because our behavior elicits a
response from them.

### Appreciation
With something as vital to a soul-mate marriage as admiration, it
is critical that we understand it—and then practice it. Admiration

involves holding someone, or something, in high regard. When we admire someone, we appreciate that person. We let him or her know, repeatedly, that he or she is important to us.

My parents, Hank and Rose, make it a point to show their appreciation to those they love. Now well into their eighties, they enjoy

...................................................................................

**THE VALUE OF APPRECIATION**
It's not just fine art and vintage cars that appreciate in value; spouses who place a premium on speaking the best of one another find their marriages soar too.

...................................................................................

more than ever hearing from friends as well as their five children.

Of the five "kids," I live the farthest away from them and subsequently don't see them as often as their other children. I am not involved in their daily lives the way my siblings are. Nonetheless, whenever I call they let me know how much they enjoy our conversations. It seems like little time has passed as they ask questions and show how much they value Christie and me.

At times while growing up, I didn't sense their appreciation. All I could see for years were their disappointments. I harbored grudges against them, pushing them away and causing unnecessary distance. Time and distance helped me see them in new, forgiving ways. As my feelings for them softened and I forgave them for their little parental quirks, my heart warmed toward them. As my heart warmed, I treated them better. As I treated them better, I rediscovered the admiration I had in my heart for them all along.

Now having related to my parents for over fifty years, I have an enduring admiration for them that has spanned times of tension and discouragement, anger, and even rebellion. Through it all I've admired them, and that has stood the test of time.

## Generosity

Admiration also involves a generosity of spirit. It means letting go of small grudges before they become unnecessarily large. It means forgiving people for not being perfect.

One of the most powerful lessons I'm learning as a husband is the power of generosity and its role in admiration. Every time Christie lets me down—and she does let me down occasionally—I try to step back and decide if the disappointment really changes anything about why I fell in love with her and still love her. I try to consider whether her "failure" is really of any importance, or whether the situation calls for me to be larger, more generous than the failure.

I also try to put myself in her shoes. Am I capable of hurting her feelings the way she hurt mine? The answer is always yes. Am I capable of forgetting something the way she forgot something that was important to me? Again, the answer is always yes. I am infinitely capable of replicating any slight I feel from her, and this understanding always renews my generosity of spirit and admiration.

Filled with a generosity of spirit, my love for her surges. My momentary feelings of distance are bridged by new feelings of admiration. She has not lost any value whatsoever in my sight as I remind myself that I love her in her totality, not just when she is completely lovely—which is most of the time!

## Building a Mosaic

I've always liked mosaics, especially those made of broken glass. There is something spiritual about a work of beauty made of broken glass. The shards of broken glass, of course, represent our brokenness. We can imagine these individual shards illustrating our points of failure, wrong choices, and impetuous decisions. They might represent times when we have slipped into being our worst, rather than our best, selves.

........................................................................

**BEAUTY IN BROKENNESS**
Soul mates recognize that even their failures,
wrong choices, and hasty decisions—when set next
to mutual respect and unconditional love—can
bring richness and growth to a marriage.

........................................................................

The artist, however, is capable of taking these misshapen pieces of sharp, broken glass and placing them together masterfully to form a mosaic. Perhaps the different colored pieces of glass form abstract art; perhaps they are placed together in such a way so as to be framed in a church window.

A full appreciation of a mosaic requires stepping back and seeing the work of art from a distance. Up close the shards are sad chunks of glass. Once something useful, they are now broken and useless. Or are they? The artist still sees light beautifully refracted through the pieces. The artist is able to rearrange the odd shapes into something meaningful.

But, again, we can see this only from a distance. From a distance the mosaic becomes beautiful. Brokenness is transformed, and admiration is renewed. Slights are overlooked or even admired. With a new perspective, we have new admiration.

After meeting with me for a year, Garth and Jana sat in my office. Garth sat across from his wife, smiling at her adoringly. There was a twinkle in his eyes as he spoke.

"I love my young bride," he said with a boyish grin, even though he'd been married to her for thirty years. "I choose my battles, and find fewer things that need to be fought about."

Jana smiled too, basking in the glow of knowing she is loved and valued.

I watched as they communicated with their eyes, their posture, and their smiles.

"You seem secure in Garth's love," I said, looking to Jana.

"Oh yes," she said, looking at me more intently. She paused as she considered her response.

"It's not that we don't have problems, as you know. But I never doubt how much he loves me. I know he wants to be with me and no one else."

"How about you, Garth? Do you feel Jana's love for you?"

"You bet I do," he said grandly. "And what's not to love?"

We all laughed.

With that we launched into another couple's session. We reviewed the progress made during the week, which I use to assist in building a bridge between partners. Couples who make progress—and note their progress—tend to gain self-confidence and trust, giving them the ability to continue to work on difficult issues.

Over the past year, Garth and Jana have worked hard to overcome some destructive patterns of behavior that threatened their marriage a year ago. While Garth could certainly be charming, he also had a tendency to either shut up or blow up, each of which had a devastating impact on their marriage.

In spite of Jana's disarming softness, she could be quite biting in her remarks, often pushing Garth well beyond his tolerance. She had little sensitivity to his need to slow down their discussions, leading him to ultimately separate from her. We've had to work to eradicate those self-destructive behaviors from their marriage.

Jana and Garth initially couldn't see many of the factors hurting their marriage. Within a relatively short time, however, they understood the importance of simultaneously rooting out their negative traits and replacing them with positive qualities.

Even as we worked to improve their communication styles, we always kept their admiration for each other front and center. I repeatedly reminded them that their marriage was a mosaic of light and dark pieces, but it could be put together into something beautiful. It was their task to see their relationship from that perspective, appreciating even the traits that at times frustrated them. Stirring up the fires of passion and admiration allowed them to keep other problems in perspective.

Garth is still head over heels in love with Jana, and she still loves him very much. I encourage them to regularly remind themselves of their passion, which so easily slips away during times of tension. They now share their admiration freely with each other.

## Abolish Criticism

I remember growing up watching my parents turn on our huge console television every time Billy Graham was on. They had a strong admiration for him, which they passed on to me. I also recall several occasions when I heard people trying to impugn Reverend Graham's character in front of my parents. They chose to ignore these smarmy rumors, cheap gossip, and general negativity.

As I watched Reverend Graham over the decades, I noted his devotion to his wife and have even met some of his children, solidifying my incredible respect and admiration for him. If even Billy Graham is criticized, it's obvious that condemnation can creep in anywhere— including a loving relationship.

That's why it's so important to abolish criticism, in all shapes and forms, from your marriage. Even hints of it in the form of exaggerated words, tone inflections, or reminders of past failures have got to be wiped out. Encouragement alone is the tool to initiate change!

Garth and Jana learned early in counseling the importance of abolishing criticism from their relationship, seeing it as a killer to intimacy.

Jana had difficulty at first seeing herself as a critical person. She rationalized her criticism because of Garth's behavior.

"If he wouldn't back away from me, abandoning me, I wouldn't criticize him," Jana said during our early work.

"But it may be precisely because of your criticism and the way you share it that he backs away," I said. "Yes, he needs to learn to be assertive with you, but he has had trouble doing that."

Garth was also critical of Jana.

"I hate the way she harps on certain issues," he said in the past. "I feel like a little boy being scolded."

Both had to learn how to ask for what they needed without using criticism. They had to learn to frame their requests in terms of prefer-

---

**FORGIVE AND FORGET**

Admiration means being generous of spirit. It means letting go of small grudges and forgiving someone for not being perfect.

---

ences, not demands. They had to learn to be direct but diplomatic, clear but loving.

In their book *Creating Optimism*, Bob Murray and Alicia Fortinberry made the following comments about "constructive" criticism: "We believe that there's no such thing. *Criticism is always about control.* If you want someone to do or not do something, you tell her very specifically what you want. If you wish to express an opinion, you use an 'I' statement and acknowledge that you are saying something about *yourself*, not about the other person."[1]

How might your behavior change if you believed all criticism was about control? How drastically might your relationship improve if you could master the art of asking for what you need? Carefully considering the wording of your request before making it can have an incredible impact on maintaining admiration for your mate.

Choose today to abolish criticism from your relationship. Make an agreement with your mate that you will outlaw gossip, stop rumors, and exemplify admiration.

## Everyone Responds to Admiration

The incredible beauty of admiration is that everyone responds favorably to it. If you want something to improve, or someone to change a certain behavior, admiration is a great tool to use.

Christie and I decided years ago that we would be a couple who emphasized admiration over criticism. We decided to intentionally choose traits that we admired in each other and make a point of commenting on them. We chose to overlook the annoying faults common in every relationship.

"I appreciate the dinner you made tonight," I say.

"I just called to tell you 'I love you,'" she says.

"I admire how hard you're working in your fitness class," I remark.

"Thanks for working really hard on the lawn this weekend," she says.

These are simple comments, but they say so much. Just as surely as criticism tears couples down, admiration and praise build them up. Just as criticism and negativity are disheartening and make us want to give up, encouragement and admiration make us want to try harder.

A commitment to mutual admiration makes it safe for both of you to be exactly who you are. In other words, admiration erases fear. Your mate doesn't have to walk on eggshells but learns to expect admiration—and slowly lets go of fear. In this safe haven, your mate is free to become the soul mate you desire.

"The gift of value is the absence of fear," says Denis Waitley. "People who live with fear grow up standing at the end of every line. People who live with praise learn to stand alone and lead their parade, even if it's raining."[2]

..........................................................................................

**THE GLUE OF ADMIRATION**
Mutual admiration will create a strong and enduring
bond between you and your spouse.

..........................................................................................

I cannot emphasize strongly enough the importance of creating this safe place to land and encouraging your mate to create a safe place for you to land. You both must know, beyond a shadow of a doubt, that your mate admires you and will let you know that. You must be able to anticipate this admiration, which feeds you as much as your daily vitamin.

While everyone responds to admiration, your comments of praise and encouragement must be specific. It's not enough to say, "I admire you." This statement is shallow and won't have the impact you desire. Instead, try these approaches:

- Make a specific comment every day about something you admire in your mate.
- Make a specific comment every day noting your understanding of how hard your mate works, in or out of the home.
- Ask questions about your mate's day and take interest in what he or she has done that day.
- Offer to help your spouse work through problems.
- Make it clear that you need your mate and are glad you are married to him or her.

Dennis and Barbara Rainey wrote a wonderful book titled *Building Your Mate's Self-Esteem*. They believe it is our responsibility to make a practice of pleasing and admiring our mates.

The Raineys suggest that pleasing our mates requires three things:

1. *Accurate knowledge.* The Raineys suggest that the best way to please your mate is simply to ask, "What could I do to please you?" While this sounds incredibly simplistic, it works. If you ask, your mate will probably respond.

2. *Sacrifice.* Your mate will determine how much you love him or her by how sacrificial you are. What are you willing to give up to show your spouse that he or she is number one in your book? Obviously, giving flowers is wonderful, but it clearly takes less sacrificial effort than arranging an evening out, babysitter included.

3. *Adventure.* Marriage was never intended to become boring, and soul mates find ways to keep their marriage exciting and adventuresome. Even when the trail gets a bit thorny, being with your soul mate makes it all worthwhile. Are you putting in energy to keep every day of your marriage interesting?[3]

This recipe for creating admiration in your marriage works. If you take the time and effort to fulfill each of these requirements, you'll enjoy the fruits of bringing out the soul mate in your mate.

## Mutual Admiration

We shouldn't be surprised that Scripture also speaks about the importance of admiration. Read these words from the apostle Paul to the church in Philippi: "Finally, brothers, whatever is true, whatever is noble, whatever is right, whatever is pure, whatever is lovely, *whatever is admirable*—if anything is excellent or praiseworthy—think about such things" (Philippians 4: 8-9, italics added).

This is incredible! The apostle Paul tells us to change the way we think. We must focus on things that are wonderful, excellent, and admirable. By changing how we think, we change who we are.

There is a famous scene in *Peter Pan*. The children have seen Peter fly, and they wish to fly too. They try different tactics—attempting to fly from the floor, from the bed, exerting all of their efforts, but the result is always the same—failure.

"How do you do it?" John asked.

And Peter answered: "You just think lovely, wonderful thoughts and they lift you up in the air."

Isn't this the truth? When we think wonderful, lovely thoughts, they lift us up. We have the ability, through God's grace, to change how we view situations. The result is either thoughts that carry us down or thoughts that lift us up.

Recently Christie and I visited my son and daughter-in-law and their baby, Caleb. We want to be as involved as possible in their lives, but as a second-year resident in surgery, my son's time is limited. Jacqueline works as well, and at times we feel like we're living out the theme of Harry Chapin's hit song "Cat's In the Cradle." With their busy schedules, Joshua and his family have little time left for us.

Dispirited at the infrequency of our visits, I began to think thoughts that were not noble, certainly were not pure, and couldn't even come close to being admirable. Fortunately, Christie challenged me to be more generous in my thinking.

"They are busy, David," she said lovingly. "We must understand their busy lives, pray for them, and take whatever times are offered to us. This is a time to support and love them, not to harbor hurt feelings."

Her words encouraged me. After our visit, I shot off an e-mail thanking them for their time and honoring their young family. I received an immediate reply from Jacqueline thanking us for coming over to see them and encouraging us to come back soon.

If there is anything worthy of praise, think about those things.

I recently read about a writers' group that, like all such groups, had meetings to which each member brought something to read aloud. However, this is where the similarity to other groups ends. This writers' group had adopted the rule of "no criticism, only admiration." For a writers' group to abolish criticism is almost absurd. Writers come expecting their work will be critiqued for the purpose, of course, of making it better.

This group, however, decided to try something different. Instead of being a "critique group," they were an "admiration group." They decided to read inspirational quotations about being artists, serving to encourage them for having the courage to write.

Instead of offering criticism, members offered only admiration and encouragement. The result? Members indicated their writing improved. Hmm.

Marriage provides many opportunities to think about admirable things. You have chances every day to catch your mate doing things worthy of admiration. Will you choose to see them?

## Mutual Admiration Society

Admiration changes us and must be included in our toolbox for bringing out the soul mates in our spouses. I am proud to be a new member of the Mutual Admiration Society (MAS). I haven't always deserved membership in this prestigious group. In fact, my request for membership was turned down several years in a row. Despite my protests that I had character worthy of membership, closer scrutiny revealed I held too much of a critical spirit to join their ranks.

Thankfully a light went on several years ago. It finally dawned on me that being critical wasn't working, while practicing admiration gave numerous benefits. With my behavior beginning to change, and my thinking more closely aligning to Philippians 4:8-9, I was finally granted membership in the MAS.

My wife and I actually formed our own chapter of the Mutual Admiration Society. In our own small society, my wife and I are intentional about noticing what is lovely, true, and admirable about others as well as ourselves. We've agreed to abolish gossip and criticism, speak the truth in love, and pay closer attention to those things that are admirable in each other, assuming others never try to intentionally hurt us.

This is a fabulous society. The only requirement is a willingness to admire the best in each other. There are no other dues or membership fees. We've abolished criticism, filtered out negativity, and agreed to speak admiration. It's pretty simple stuff and unbelievably powerful in changing lives and marriages.

Membership in the Mutual Admiration Society requires the one thing many people have difficulty enacting: filtering out negativity. What does this mean? It means refusing to get involved in petty arguments, choosing instead to believe the best about a person.

The apostle Paul encourages us to celebrate our mates' progress rather than carp on their weaknesses. We must notice where they need encouragement and then generously offer it. We must never focus on where they struggle but instead amplify their strengths.

There are countless benefits to living in the Mutual Admiration Society:

1. We give our mates the courage and strength to pursue their interests and goals.
2. We create an environment in which our mates can encourage us to dream and live out our goals.
3. We create a place of safety where our mates feel free to be who they are.
4. We are given permission by our mates to be who we are.
5. We create a place where we can open up and share more of our gifts and lives with each other.
6. We receive admiration from our spouses.
7. We create an atmosphere where anxiety gives way to laughter, where peace and joy thrive.

If you have ever lived in a Mutual Admiration Society, you'll never want to live anywhere else. Once you feel the daily encouragement, trust, and boundless love found in those surroundings, you'll never want to slip back into a critical space. Having felt prized and adored, you'll never settle for anything less.

## Weekly Quiz

There is power in admiration. We're all hungry for it, and our mates, perhaps more than anyone else, deserve it. Consider making admiration a habit you weave into the tapestry of your marriage. You'll love the results.

Practicing admiration can be hard. How might you handle this situation:

You've spent Thanksgiving Day at your sister's house, eating turkey and watching football with a dozen other relatives. As you drive away, you

    a) dissect your family members' behavior, criticizing aspects of each person.

    b) compliment your spouse on how masterfully he handled the challenges of the evening, thanking him for his support.

## PUTTING IT INTO PRACTICE THIS WEEK

1. If you were to build a mosaic that represented your marriage, what scenes would you include? How have the smooth, colorful pieces enriched your life? How have the dark, jagged pieces added depth and compassion to your soul?

2. Take time, ideally as a couple, to look back over the 12 steps to a soul mate marriage (see pages xvi–xviii in the prologue). Identify the areas in which you've grown, as well as those you'd like to continue working on.

3. As you end this study, sit down—with your spouse, if possible—and complete the following sentences:

    • I have hope for our marriage because:

    • I appreciate the way that you:

    • I admire you because:

    • I want to _____ for you.

    • I want to take time to _____ together.

    • My dream for our marriage is:

*Afterword*

# THE DECISION

We have reached the end of our journey together. I've been a silent witness to your courage to revolutionize your marriage by choosing to bring out the soul mate in your mate.

We've traveled together for twelve weeks—just enough time to learn and practice twelve incredibly valuable skills, each woven together to form a foolproof formula for bringing out the soul mate in your mate. Of course you haven't completely mastered these skills yet, but you have begun the journey. Each tool, every strategy, is meant to be used time and again. As you do so, you'll notice amazing results.

If you've begun practicing some of the tools in this book, you know results are possible. You may have already had moments of giddiness, laughter, finishing each other's sentences, and knowing what your mate thinks and wants. You've felt the closeness that is enjoyed only by soul mates.

Everything, however, hinges on a decision. Will you choose to bring out the soul mate in your mate? Conventional wisdom says to wait until he or she is a soul mate to you and then offer something in return. This simply doesn't work.

You have the power to set positive or negative patterns into motion. If you choose patterns of positive action, you'll be encouraged, and your mate will be as well. You will be enlivened and so will your mate. By choosing to be a soul mate, as well as bringing the soul mate out in your mate, you'll be in for a lifetime of passion and romance.

Everything hinges on your decision to initiate being a soul mate and, moreover, your ability to bring out the soul mate in your mate. Do you have the vision?

Choose to practice the strategies offered in this book—they're powerful and they work. Trust me. My marriage has had non-soul-mate moments and plenty of soul mate moments, and I much prefer the latter. I have found, unquestionably, that I determine whether or not

Christie is my soul mate. As I do my part in bringing out the soul mate in her, I am blessed with her being a magnificent soul mate to me.

You must make a rock-solid decision to continue on this journey. Review the chapter summaries, deciding to practice these tools, making them habits in your life. You must decide you're going to admire and appreciate your mate. Even when you notice qualities not fitting a soul mate, look deeper. Try harder. Pursue something more. There is a soul mate waiting for you, right in the middle of your marriage.

There are no perfect people, and certainly no perfect marriages. Fortunately, being a soul mate does not depend on being perfect. It depends only on being real, being classy, and being committed to a vision for what is possible. Like the spectacular mosaic of broken pieces, you can choose to see your mate for who he or she is—a soul mate. It is your decision and task to bring out the soul mate in your mate. God bless you in your journey.

# NOTES

**WEEK 1: REEVALUATING YOUR PERSPECTIVE**
1. Daniel Goleman, *Emotional Intelligence* (New York: Bantam Books, 1995), 114.

**WEEK 2: CHOOSING ROSE-COLORED GLASSES**
1. William Bridges, *Transitions* (Cambridge, MA.: Perseus Publishing, 2001), 85.
2. Donald Clarke, *A Marriage After God's Own Heart* (Sisters, OR: Multnomah Publishers, 2001), 183.
3. Daphne Rose Kingma, *True Love* (Berkeley, CA: Conari Press, 2002), 37.
4. Rosamund Stone Zander and Benjamin Zander, *The Art of Possibility* (New York: Penguin Books, 2000), 9.

**WEEK 3: BRINGING OUT THE BEST QUALITIES OF YOUR SPOUSE**
1. Julia Cameron, *The Artist's Way* (New York: Jeremy P. Tarcher/Putnam, 1992), 91.
2. Alexandra Stoddard, *Gracious Living in a New World* (New York: William Morrow & Co., 1996), 46.

**WEEK 4: REMEMBERING THE REASONS YOUR MATE LOVES YOU**
1. Thomas Moore, *Soul Mates* (New York: HarperCollins Publishers, 1994), 11.
2. Kahlil Gibran, *The Prophet* (New York: Alfred A. Knopf, 1923), 15.

**WEEK 5: GIVING UP DISTRACTIONS TO THE DREAM**
1. Robert Paul, *Finding Ever After* (Minneapolis: Bethany House Publishers, 2007), 26.
2. Frances G. Wickes, *The Inner World of Choices* (New York: Harper & Row, 1963), 64–65.
3. Adele Ahlberg Calhoun, *Spiritual Disciplines Handbook* (Downers Grove, IL: InterVarsity Press, 2005), 97.
4. Michael Gurian, *Love's Journey* (Boston: Shambhala, 1995).
5. Scott Peck, *The Road Less Traveled* (New York: Touchstone, 1978).

**WEEK 6: EMBRACING THE RIPPLE EFFECT**
1. Seth Godin, *Purple Cow* (New York: Penguin Group, 2002), 31–32.
2. Malcolm Gladwell, *The Tipping Point* (New York: Little, Brown & Co., 2000), 5.
3. Laura Schlessinger, *The Proper Care and Feeding of Marriage* (New York: Harper, 2007), 191.
4. David Schwartz, *The Magic of Thinking Big* (New York: Simon & Schuster, 1959), 106.

**WEEK 7: NURTURING YOUR MATE'S DREAMS**
1. Sherry Suib Cohen, *Secrets of a Very Good Marriage* (New York: Carol Southern Books, 1993), 132.
2. Daniel Pink, *A Whole New Mind: Moving from the Information Age to the Conceptual Age* (New York: Riverhead Books, 2005), 159.
3. Irwin Kula, *Yearnings* (New York: Hyperion, 2006), 188–189.
4. Matthew Kelly, *The Seven Levels of Intimacy* (New York: Simon & Schuster, 2005), 56–57.

**WEEK 8: TEACHING YOUR MATE TO NURTURE YOUR DREAMS**
1. Dag Hammarskjöld, *Markings* (New York: Alfred A. Knopf, 1969), 13.
2. To find out more about morning pages, see Julia Cameron's book *The Artist's Way*, 9–18.
3. Ed Wheat, *Love Life for Every Married Couple* (New York: HarperCollins, 1980), 133.

**WEEK 9: PREPARING YOUR BEST TO MEET YOUR SPOUSE'S BEST**

1. P. M. Forni, *The Civility Solution* (New York: St. Martin's Press, 2008).
2. Thomas Moore, *Soul Mates*, 30–32.
3. Susan Baur, *The Love of Your Life* (Naperville, IL: Sourcebooks, Inc., 2002), 88–89.
4. Ibid., 91.
5. Ibid., 90.

**WEEK 10: UNLEASHING THE POWER OF POSITIVE GOSSIPING**

1. See http://gossipfree.org for more information.
2. Rosamund Stone Zander and Benjamin Zander, *The Art of Possibility*, 125.
3. Peggy Klaus, *Brag!* (New York: Warner Business Books, 2000), 2–3.
4. Ibid., 5.
5. Stephen Covey, *The 7 Habits of Highly Effective People* (New York: Simon & Schuster, 1989), 239.
6. Sarah Ban Breathnach, *Simple Abundance* (New York: Warner Books, 1995). This quote appears in the entry for April 5.
7. Julia Cameron, *The Artist's Way*, 110.

**WEEK 11: INITIATING CHANGE BY ENCOURAGEMENT**

1. Harville Hendrix, *Keeping the Love You Find* (New York: Simon & Schuster, 1992), 288.
2. Thomas Moore, *Soul Mates*, 255.
3. Stephanie Dowrick, *Forgiveness & Other Acts of Love* (New York: W. W. Norton & Co., 1997), 185.
4. John Gottman, *Why Marriages Succeed or Fail* (New York: Simon & Schuster, 1994), 73.
5. Lewis Losoncy, *If It Weren't for You, We Could Get Along* (Sanford, FL: DC Press, 2001), 52.

**WEEK 12: MAINTAINING MUTUAL ADMIRATION**

1. Bob Murray and Alicia Fortinberry, *Creating Optimism* (New York: McGraw-Hill, 2004), 95; italics in original.
2. Denis Waitley, *Seeds of Greatness* (Old Tappan, NJ: Fleming H. Revell, 1983), 41.
3. Dennis and Barbara Rainey, *Building Your Mate's Self-Esteem* (Nashville: Thomas Nelson, 1985).

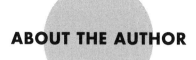

# ABOUT THE AUTHOR

Dr. David Hawkins has been counseling for over thirty years and is the author of more than thirty books, including the best-selling series, Your Pocket Therapist. He is also the weekly advice columnist for both Crosswalk.com and CBN.com. Dr. Hawkins founded the Marriage Recovery Center and owns Pacific Psychological Associates with offices located throughout Washington State. He lives on Bainbridge Island, Washington, with his wife, Christie. Visit him online at http://www.yourrelationshipdoctor.com.